Rosie the Rubber Worker

Women Workers in
Akron's Rubber Factories
During World War II

Kathleen L. Endres

**The Kent State
University Press**

Kent, Ohio, & London

© 2000 by The Kent State University Press, Kent, Ohio 44242

ALL RIGHTS RESERVED

Library of Congress Catalog Card Number 00-035219

ISBN 0-87338-667-1

Manufactured in the United States of America

07 06 05 04 03 02 01 00   5 4 3 2 1

Frontispiece: An unidentified woman at BFG works assembling a life vest.
B. F. Goodrich Collection.

Library of Congress Cataloging-in-Publication Data
Endres, Kathleen L.
Rosie the Rubber Worker : women workers in Akron's rubber factories during
World War II / Kathleen L. Endres.
p.   cm.
Includes bibliographical references and index.
ISBN 0-87338-667-1 (cloth : alk. paper) ∞
1. Women rubber industry workers—Ohio—Akron—History. 2. Women rubber
industry workers—Ohio—Akron—Interviews. 3. Women—Employment—Ohio—
Akron—History. 4. World War, 1939–1945 x Women—Ohio—Akron—History.
I. Title.
HD6073.R9 U623 2000
331.4'8783'097713609044—dc21   00-035219

British Library Cataloging-in-Publication data are available.

Rosie the Rubber Worker

contents

one

Introducing Rosie

Rosie the Riveter" was a familiar image during World War II, an affable, attractive, young miss who went to work in a factory for patriotic reasons and made the products America needed to wage war. She left the trappings of femininity at home—the stockings, the pumps, the frills. She donned the clothes she needed to get the job done—comfortable shoes, trousers, and work shirt. Her hair was neatly tucked beneath a handkerchief. Rosie always seemed to have the right attitude, as the frequently cited motto, "We can do it!" attested. But underneath the work clothes and bandanna lurked a woman who looked forward to returning to the kitchen and taking care of her husband and children.

Rosie the Riveter was an image created by the government and industry to help recruit women into the factories during World War II. The historian Maureen Honey outlined the many groups involved with creating Rosie, the image. The War Advertising Council, which represented many leaders of the advertising industry, was among the first groups formed. The council was involved in many campaigns, but its "Women in the War" program of 1944 is the most famous. In that campaign, the council asked advertisers to address the theme of women production workers and even suggested the most appropriate appeals.

The Office of War Information's Bureau of Campaigns contacted the news, motion picture, graphics, magazine, and radio bureaus to mount a concerted effort. Some of the bureaus sent out story ideas, provided background facts, and helped arrange news tours. The campaign was

not just limited to the print media. The "new" women industrial workers also became radio personalities.

Rubber companies—and their corporate aircraft affiliates—used their women workers to reinforce the Rosie image in a variety of advertisements, posters, news campaigns, and radio broadcasts. These campaigns applauded the role of women workers in rubber production and their commitment to the war effort.

Posters were either issued by the rubber companies or reproduced in the company newspapers. B. F. Goodrich (BFG), for example, reproduced one poster in its *War Production News* in which a woman was quoted as saying, "I've got a date with VICTORY! So I'll stick to my own little job until the big job is done!" The caption read: "This lass above seems to know that a few pleasures may have to be given up for the duration of

(*Opposite*) If only one illustration captures the image of the working women in wartime America, it is "Rosie the Riveter." This patriotic young woman went to work in industry to help make the products necessary to wage war and thereby bring the men home more quickly. Rosie—in all her various forms—was an image created by government and industry to recruit and retain women in war jobs. *Courtesy of the National Archives.*

Advertising was used not only to get women on the job but also to keep them there. The rubber companies' periodicals often carried advertising that was designed to keep women at work. This advertisement appeared in BFG's *War Production News*, April 9, 1942. *B. F. Goodrich Collection, University of Akron Archives.*

B. F. Goodrich and other rubber companies featured production women in advertising during World War II. This advertisement shows a woman inspecting intravenous tubing. It appeared in *Newsweek*, *Time*, and *Business Week* in August and September 1943. *B. F. Goodrich Collection.*

the war, for it is a hard war and she needed to win it. She knows that she must replace a man who has joined Uncle Sam's fighting forces. And she knows that even if she should get married during the present manpower crisis, she should stay with the job if at all possible until victory." The company's newspaper also reproduced at least one poster from the "This is *My* war!" series. It showed women making pontoons, one product that many female rubber workers made in Akron during World War II.

Not every poster gave such a clear message. In its poster congratulating the workers who made the life raft that saved Captain Eddie Rickenbacker, Goodyear pictured only male workers, even though women workers were heavily involved in life-raft production. Under the headline, "Our work sure means something when it saves Rickenbacker and his companions," two workers—a woman, Flossie Anson, and a man, E. K. Brown—were quoted: "We're builders in the life raft department at Goodyear where the life rafts that saved Captain Rickenbacker and his crew mates were built. Their rescue certainly gave all of our life raft builders a big thrill; made us feel we really were in there pitching in this man's war." Rickenbacker was rescued after being missing at sea for five weeks aboard one of Goodyear's life rafts. The workers quoted in that ad continued: "Guess that's pretty good proof that when we cement a seam [typically a woman's job] we do it for keeps. Now we've a picture of 'Rick' and his raft hanging in the shop. It's a reminder that we're helping save the lives of our boys out there. It makes our whole crew feel mighty proud of their work and its importance."

Women were also featured in rubber company advertising. BFG introduced "Mrs. Sherlock Holmes," whose job was to inspect seals. This "trained woman inspector" threw out the seals that might endanger the lives of the servicemen aboard airplanes. Highlighting the competent woman inspectors was a favorite theme in BFG's wartime advertising. In "War job: watching the glowing tubes," BFG proclaimed: "So women who are trained tubing experts are busy watching, foot by foot, the many miles of extra tubing needed now to meet war needs. It's a rubber improvement that will help save lives of soldiers or civilians—in peace as well as war time."

Another communication form, which had a much longer life, was the brochure and booklet produced either by the rubber company itself or by its trade organization, the Rubber Manufacturers Association. *The Rubber Industry and the War* showed women hastening victory by working in factories. *All Out for Victory at Firestone* showed many women workers, some working with men. But none could compare with the powerful message of Seaman Elgin Staples and his mother, Vera Mueller, who worked in the company's Life Belt Division. A Firestone life belt had saved the sailor's life when his ship was sunk in the South Pacific.

Newspapers, magazines, and wire services sent reporters and editors to tour the rubber plants and interview the women workers. In 1943, Goodyear Aircraft was on the itinerary for the Aviation Writers Tour; in 1942, a "Camera Caravan" visited Firestone. A *Philadelphia Inquirer* reporter wrote about the women who made barrage balloons; *Nation's Business* showed how women were taking over men's jobs as tire builders.

Women were prominently featured when celebrities came to the rubber factories. After vocalist and band leader Xavier Cugat visited Firestone, the photo in the company's newspaper pictured Cugat with Harvey Firestone, son of the founder, and a woman factory worker, Mrs. Robert Mikesell. War heroes also reinforced the image of Rosie by meeting with the women workers and thanking them for their work. Seaman Basil Dominic Izzi, survivor of eighty-three days on board a raft in the Atlantic, told the women—six of whom were pictured—to keep up the good work. "One of these rafts may save your father, your husband or your brother," he assured the women at BFG.

The most articulate women found themselves on the radio. Such opportunities were limited and generally reserved for "special" workers. Mary Snader was the first woman to build airplane tires for Firestone.

Women production workers at Goodyear Aviation were the darlings of the press corps. Here a woman worker demonstrates riveting techniques to a woman journalist who was part of the Aviation Writers Tour of 1943. Photos like this one romanticized the image of Rosie not only in the local papers but also across the nation. *Goodyear Collection, University of Akron Archives.*

Women did not have to be riveters to be showcased on press tours. In the 1943 Aviation Writers Tour, a woman production worker at Goodyear Aircraft demonstrates production to men writers. *Goodyear Collection.*

For that accomplishment, she was honored at the Second War Congress of American Industry in New York City; while there, she was scheduled to speak on Adelaide Hawley's radio show on WEAF.

The female rubber worker was even more prominent locally, in the company publications and the city newspapers. Nonetheless, these women all seemed to have much in common with the image of Rosie: most were young women who joined the industrial workforce for patriotic reasons and planned to leave their jobs as soon as the war was over. But as long as the nation was at war and their men were away, the women would work hard to bring their loved ones home.

To that end, Goodyear initiated "The Real Miss Americas" series, which profiled female industrial workers (and, to a lesser extent, office workers). Leila Fletcher, who joined Goodyear on April 1, 1943, after her husband left for the service, said: "I have found the work [at Goodyear Tire and Rubber] very interesting and I enjoy doing it. Of course, it's just a duration job and, like hundreds of other war wives, I'm looking forward to the day when I can again settle down to being a housewife."

Evelyn Haidnich was another Goodyear Miss America. She started at the company after she graduated from Akron's East High School in 1940. The next year she married and had an even greater reason for working hard: "I like working in the belt room and only hope that in some way the small part I am playing in war production may assure better operation of a machine that is making some vital product to the army that will help bring my husband home just a bit sooner."

Ruth Milligan Dietrick said that she had three reasons for working hard in Goodyear's life-raft department: her daughters (Marjorie, five, and June, twelve) and son (Jene, five). "When victory comes to our country and our allies[,] I shall consider my war work done and devote my entire time to my family. Until that time I shall put every ounce of energy at my disposal to help defeat Hitler and his gang," she told a reporter for the company's newspaper.

Firestone's *Non-Skid* and BFG's *War Production News* reinforced the image of Rosie through profiles of female rubber workers as well. Firestone's Margaret Graham was typical. She started at Firestone as a riveter when her husband went off to war. Her job kept her from worrying about her husband constantly: "She doesn't have time to worry about him when she is driving rivets," the company reporter observed. At the same time, she was saving for their future together. "From the time when she is just 'Mrs.' again, Private and Mrs. Graham have plans so Margaret says she is saving as much as possible now to make those plans materialize."

Afton Hill, who worked in Department 6535, wanted it understood

Rallies in Akron sustained the morale of the city during the war, encouraged the sale of "victory bonds," upheld the morale of the women workers because they featured products produced primarily by females, and acted as recruitment tools for additional workers, especially women, who attended. *Goodyear Collection.*

that she was working to help get her husband home and thought all other married women should do likewise. "I'm working because I think everyone should work now to win this war. I have a husband in the Marines overseas and a brother in Africa, and I wouldn't feel right if I didn't work and help them all I could. Here I feel that I really am doing something to win the war." Katherine Juhasz, of materials control in Department 2501, felt the same way: "I'm working because my husband is in the service and I want to have a part in defeating the Axis. I felt that I was able to do a job in the war effort, and I decided it would be unpatriotic not to do it." Only Pauline Rohrbaugh, of fuel cells in Department 7614, admitted that money entered into her decision to go to work at BFG. "I'm working because I need the job to support myself and because I think everyone should work now to help win the war."

The *Akron Beacon Journal*, the city's daily newspaper, carried much the same message; women of all ages and classes worked primarily for

patriotic reasons and would gladly return home in peacetime. Mildred Wilcox went into Goodyear's tube room when her two sons, Thomas and Donald, went to war. "I felt that I should help too," she told the *Beacon* reporter. "I'm staying on my job until the war is won and my boys come home again. Then I'm going to spend all my time cooking and keeping house." The *Akron Beacon Journal* reports emphasized the middle- to upper-middle-class women workers. Among those being trained as prospective aircraft inspectors were Mary Rusinko, wife of the Summit County deputy recorder; Lucy Stevens, wife of Judge Perry Stevens; Pauline Bledsoe, who had attended Ohio State University and

The young and old, women and men, office and production workers stream into work at B. F. Goodrich during World War II. They always passed posters urging them to buy bonds, stay on the job, and produce to maximum efficiency. One poster pictured reminded the workers, "Your Job Is Vital to Victory!" *B. F. Goodrich Collection.*

Many rubber companies had problems keeping women on the job. Signs such as this one at Goodyear were frequently posted at the workplace as constant reminders to women to keep them on the job. *Cleveland Press Collection, Cleveland State University.*

Heidelberg College; and Mrs. Gomer Morgan, fifty-one, who came from Uhrichsville to work with her daughter Jeanne, nineteen, who had the "wanderlust" and decided to work at Goodyear Aircraft.

In such stories, defense training became the great class equalizer. As one *Beacon* reporter emphasized in 1942, "There are college graduates in this school and there are school teachers. There are barmaids and waitresses and former shoe clerks and rubber workers and maids. There are bored West Hill housewives and there are daughters of some of the people whose names make the society pages." All, however, were united in a single goal—speeding the end of the war; the society matron and the girl from Appalachia became a team.

The newspaper stories, the advertisements, and the broadcasts all provided a wonderful public image. But these images do not reflect the reality of the women who worked in Akron's rubber factories very closely.

Unlike many industries that hired women only during wartime, Akron's rubber industry had a long history of employing women in production jobs.

The history of women in the rubber industry dates back to well before World War II and the patriotic appeals and the image of Rosie and even back to before the rubber companies moved to Akron in the late nineteenth century. Women were probably first introduced to rubber factory production more because of geography than because of something special about the industry itself. Charles Goodyear, who made the rubber industry possible because of his invention of the vulcanization process, was a native of New England, then the center of rubber production. New England, with its long history of textile manufacturing,

The absenteeism problem was especially acute in 1943 as the rubber companies pushed to make their production quotas. This cartoon reminded the women that the jobs they did in the factory had direct connection to the war effort. War Production News, *October 22, 1943*. *B. F. Goodrich Collection.*

had long relied on women as a primary labor supply. Unable to finance rubber production himself, Goodyear sold patents at relatively low rates to manufacturers in the area. Goodyear thought up hundreds of uses for rubber, many of which could be categorized as mechanical rubber goods. They included everything from rubber bands to engine hoses. Production of these small items emphasized manual dexterity rather than physical strength—the very qualities women workers were noted for. Rubber also made its way into the boot and shoe industry, which had long employed women.

When B. F. Goodrich came to Akron in 1870 in search of a new location for his rubber company, Akron had neither the labor power nor the manufacturing base to pose much of a threat to cities in New England or anywhere else. Akron had only a modest population of 10,006, but it did have its good points, at least from Goodrich's perspective. The city had an adequate transportation system (the Ohio Canal and railroads already cut through the city); it offered a variety of relatively inexpensive sites that allowed for expansion; a group of local entrepreneurs seemed able to help out if—when—Goodrich ran into trouble; and there was a large enough labor supply to get the rubber factory going. And so, in 1870, B. F. Goodrich settled on a site beyond Exchange Street, near Lock One on the Ohio Canal. There rose the first rubber manufacturing company west of the Alleghenies.

Until Goodrich came to town, few of Akron's industries offered jobs to women. Flour and cereal milling brought prosperity to the city—but few jobs for women. Clay deposits around the city spawned another industry, but the kilns and potteries needed many men but few women workers. Akron became a center for farm-implement manufacture, but few women were needed there. The only promising new industry for female workers was match production.

When Goodrich opened his factory, he planned to concentrate on producing fire hoses. Goodrich explained, "Leather hose is apt to spring a leak, or burst, just when you need it most. I'd make the best fire hose in the world, and go from there into other lines." His company quickly diversified its product line. Hard rubber and molded goods were added in 1881; surgeons' gloves and dry sundries in 1887; bicycle tires in the 1880s. By the 1890s, BFG's biggest sellers were bicycle tires, hoses, drug sundries, and molded goods. The next century would find the company going into the manufacture of boots and shoes. Many of these early departments relied heavily on women production workers.

Goodrich's success in Akron brought a flood of imitators. Miller Rubber was organized in 1892 to manufacture druggist sundries. O. C. Barber, the "match king," tried his hand with the Diamond Rubber Company. Goodyear Tire and Rubber opened in 1898 with little capital but with enlightened management, especially once P. W. Litchfield joined the company as the superintendent in 1900. That same year, Firestone came to Akron. Nonetheless, census reports at that time showed that Ohio ranked only fourth in rubber and elastic goods manufacturing, behind Massachusetts, New Jersey, and Connecticut. Ohio was also fourth in rubber boot and shoe manufacturing. Massachusetts was number one in that industry too.

But in Akron rubber production was just getting started. Soon Kelly-Springfield, Mohawk, Marathon Tire, Falls Rubber, Lambert, Mason, Amazon, Star, American, India, and General opened factories in the city or one of the neighboring communities. The new companies, as well as the larger ones established during the previous century, brought Akron boom years between 1910 and 1920.

At the end of the nineteenth century, the big rubber product line was bicycle tires, whose manufacturing increased with the national cycling craze. In the twentieth century, however, the major product line for many of these rubber companies would be automobile tires, which fed a new demand. Automobile tire production was heavy, dirty work—men's work, well-paid men's work. Understandably, the rubber industry and the automobile industry became vitally linked. Tire production brought enormous prosperity to certain companies. Four companies—three of them based in Akron—emerged as the leading rubber manufacturers in the nation. Akron's contributions to the Big Four were B. F. Goodrich, Firestone Tire and Rubber, and Goodyear Tire and Rubber. The other, the United States Rubber Company, had been formed in 1892 with the consolidation of nine manufacturers of rubber boots and shoes and incorporated in New Jersey.

Had the rubber factories produced only automobile tires, there would have been little room for women. But B. F. Goodrich had a diversified product line well before it got into automobile tire production, and in 1913, Goodyear introduced a line of mechanical goods. The Big Three, though the largest employers in Akron's rubber industry, were not the only ones to offer lines of goods tailor-made for female production workers. A number of smaller rubber companies did specialize in mechanical goods or toys manufactured by female laborers.

The growth in the rubber industry meant growth for Akron: population went from 16,512 in 1880, to 27,601 in 1890, to 42,728 in 1900, to 69,067 in 1910, to 208,435 in 1920, and 255,040 in 1930. Women and men were immigrating to the city, in no small part because of the jobs in the rubber factories. The pay was good, among the highest in the state, and the rubber companies were recruiting workers. Moreover, the rubber companies came to be known for their enlightened management. The Big Three were introducing innovations designed to improve the workers' status in the factories. Before 1920, the biggest rubber companies introduced on-site restaurants and hospitals. Hiring and firing were taken out of the hands of the foremen and given to a labor department. Foremen and supervisors were better trained. The largest companies shifted to an eight-hour day. Goodyear introduced an Industrial Assembly—a representative body elected by those employed in the factory—which gave the workers some form of input into management.

Some of these innovations had first been introduced—or mandated by state law—to apply to women only. For example, a shorter day was initially legislated as part of Ohio's protective labor laws for women, and on-site restaurants were initially introduced as a benefit for women workers.

Like many of the factories in the nation, Akron's rubber companies benefitted from large World War I contracts. To fill these, more workers were needed. Thus, more women were brought into the rubber factories; a few of them even took over men's jobs. In a sense, World War I became Akron's dress rehearsal for World War II production and problems.

Like many other parts of the country, Akron suffered a major economic downturn in 1920. Most companies laid off workers and slashed wages. The effect was most devastating at Goodyear, which was reorganized and had its original founders, the Seiberlings, forced out. By 1921, however, the rubber industry—and Akron—was beginning to recover.

The rest of the 1920s brought good times and prosperity to the rubber companies and to the city of Akron. Even the shutdown of large plants—the Webster, Camp and Lane division of Wellman-Seaver-Morgan, International Harvester, and Whitman and Barnes—failed to dampen the city's optimism. Other plants—primarily rubber factories—absorbed many of the laid-off workers.

The good times of the 1920s were shattered in 1929 with the stock market crash. During the Great Depression, tens of thousands of Akron workers were laid off. The rubber companies were especially devastated; payrolls at the Akron plants dropped from 58,316 to 33,285 workers.

World War II revived the rubber industry, as huge contracts for war materials flooded the city. These contracts were for not only war materials commonly associated with the rubber industry but also for aircraft parts. Shortly before the war, both Firestone and Goodyear had gotten involved in aircraft production. All the rubber companies, including these new aircraft initiatives, needed workers—and not just men. More women worked in the rubber factories and their sister aircraft plants than ever before. Rosie the Rubber Worker had arrived.

Rosie, however, was the third generation of women to go to work in Akron's rubber factories. Thus, from the very start, Rosie the Rubber Worker differed from the image of Rosie the Riveter. Women in the rubber factories were likely to have had factory experience. The conditions they faced, the militancy they embraced, and the industrial culture they fashioned did not fit neatly into the wartime image. Rosie typically had worked either in industry or in some service occupation before she got her job at BFG, Goodyear, Firestone, or one of Akron's smaller rubber companies.

The largest number of these women applied at the rubber companies because these factories offered them higher wages than they could earn elsewhere. All of these women wanted the war to end; all wanted their loved ones to come home. But most of women who worked in the factories needed the money for survival, for supporting their families, or for beginning a new life.

Rosie was also responsible for much of her own involvement in this industry. Rosie, her family, and her friends were key recruiters for labor into the rubber factories. Although the companies sent recruiters to the small towns in Ohio and into the neighboring states and although the companies and the government agencies advertised extensively in Akron and in other communities, the women workers themselves were one of the most important recruitment tools the rubber companies possessed.

Once on the job, women discovered that the factory was an industrial patriarchy. Most continued to hold "women's jobs" or only part of the men's jobs. The women who held men's jobs, earning men's wages, were the exception rather than the rule. Gender segmentation was also evident in management. The greatest number of supervisory positions were held by white males. The only supervisory jobs open to women were those in female-only departments.

Women were also effectively excluded from union leadership positions. Although they had been important in the development of the United Rubber Workers (URW) and were members of the union before the war (and would continue to be so after the war), women held few positions above the level of committeewoman. The exclusion of women from management, supervision, and union offices meant that the female workers had little protection except on issues that would directly affect male workers after the war. This does not mean that women lacked control over their jobs or their lives in the factory. Far from it: they created their own work environment, their own culture, through their network of friends and relatives.

Women who could adjust to the conditions in the rubber factory earned more than any other female industrial worker in Ohio. Those who could not adjust registered their dissatisfaction in different ways. Rates of absenteeism were at an all-time high, as were the turnover rates for female workers.

World War II, however, did bring one permanent change to the woman rubber worker. African American women were introduced into production jobs for the first time. Like white women, African American women came to the factory to work for the money. Their integration into production was not always smooth, but the factory environment—as defined by women—did include black women.

Rosie of the rubber factories found that Akron could be either a socially liberating or constrictive environment, depending upon one's age and marital status. It appears that the married Rosies who worked in the rubber factories were still expected to carry out all their traditional domestic duties, even though they worked forty-eight hours a week outside the home. They retained primary housekeeping responsibilities, shopping duties, and child care obligations. If they needed help, the women were likely to find it from their families or friends rather than the community, the union, or the factory management. There were some community nods to the women in the workplace, such as the Metropolitan Housing Authority day-care centers. And the extended Monday-evening shopping hours reflected the economic effect women workers had on the retailers of the city.

Single women found Akron a more liberating environment than did their married counterparts. They had the money to frequent the movies, the restaurants, the bars, and the nightclubs. Newspapers reported that the factory women were smoking and drinking. Single women from outside the city—or those living apart from their families—found that the anonymity of a metropolitan area allowed them to experience new adventures and test the boundaries of social acceptability. But once they married, they were expected to return to more traditional behaviors.

In the popular image of Rosie, women looked forward to leaving the job after the war was done. The reality, though, was much more complicated: in Akron's rubber factories, conversion took place in stages—beginning as early as 1943, when the large rubber companies began shifting certain jobs (the largest number of which were done by women) out of the city—and usually out of the state. Thus, there was not a single conversion, but rather waves of conversions. By far the hardest hit of these women were those who took jobs in the rubber company's newest venture—aircraft production. Immediately after the war, the largest number of these women workers were laid off.

In the regular rubber factories, women who held what were considered men's jobs were removed immediately from those spots. No matter how short-handed the rubber factories were for tire builders, women were not brought back into jobs that they held during the war, nor did the union press their claims. In contrast, the workers employed in "women's jobs" were sheltered at least for a time, and women rubber workers were particularly protected when the companies returned to the six-hour day.

After the war, a group of women voluntarily left their jobs to return to their homes. It is this group that most closely resembles the image of Rosie. Another group was laid off, involuntarily returning to their homes or to lesser-paying jobs outside the rubber industry. A third group stayed on, eager to continue as rubber workers.

two

Generations of Rosies

In 1905 Anna Connor became "forelady" of BFG's boot and shoe department. It was a new venture for BFG, but the company seemed confident it would have a promising future—and Anna would be part of that future. In 1913, the boot and shoe department was still going strong; but, like most of the rubber factories in Akron, BFG was shut down by the bitter Industrial Workers of the World (IWW) strike. Many of the women workers in Connor's department walked off the job. They complained that the rate for piecework assured them extremely low wages and that the working conditions were unhealthy. Testifying on behalf of BFG at hearings during the strike, Anna insisted that in her department women workers were well treated from the time they were hired. She admitted that while learning the job, single women made ten cents an hour but married women were paid by the piece. The married women were paid less, Anna explained, because they didn't stay on the job as long. "It doesn't pay the company to teach them," she said. After women were trained, all were paid on a piece rate. Most women workers did well under the system, making $1.35 to $1.40 a day after six months. None of the women in Anna's department had ever complained to her about the smell of benzene, which was regularly used in the rubber production process, or sore throats from soapstone. And, addressing complaints about ventilation, Anna insisted that BFG had the finest ventilation system of any factory in the country.

Mildred Young was part of the second generation of women who came to work in the rubber companies in Akron. She had been born

Mildred Homan on June 13, 1900, in Zoar Station, a small town not far from Canton. She and her twin moved to Akron to work for an aunt who managed a restaurant. That worked out fine until the twins turned eighteen and started looking for better-paying jobs. Mildred's sister got a job at a boardinghouse near Plant One and Mildred went to work at Goodyear Tire and Rubber in 1918. A man from the employment office came out to the street "and asked people if they would like to work for Goodyear and if they would want a job," she remembered. That sounded appealing so Mildred applied and was quickly hired to manufacture an important war product—gas masks. Mildred made more money than her sister and liked her new job. But it wasn't a job that would last for a long time—at least not initially. World War I was winding down and four months later Mildred found herself unemployed. Mildred stayed in the city, got married, and had three sons. In 1933, with three young children at home, Mildred returned to Goodyear to work in the department that made garden hoses. It was a horrible job. Mildred remembered, "I didn't care much for that job because it was too noisy. The first chance I got, I went to the tube room at Plant One." That was one of her favorite jobs. "I worked there [in the tube room] long enough to know everything that had to be done. I was always treated right by the supervisors." She worked throughout much of the Depression but remembered being laid off more than once. She honored the strike in 1936, more out of fear than anything else. She went to work the day the strike started, but someone from the company locked the conveyor and said, "'Don't you dare touch that.'" Mildred explained, "Well, I was too scared to touch anything," and she left the plant. She stayed out until the long, bitter strike was finally settled. She remembered that wages increased once the United Rubber Workers started representing the workers. When World War II came, Mildred started making war products. She assembled the kits to repair rubber boats and worked on self-sealing gas tanks. She continued at Goodyear until 1962, when she retired after twenty-six years of service.

Anna and Mildred had much in common—they went to work in the factories to earn more money than they could in most other jobs in the city and they developed a strong sense of community within their departments. They also found an industrial patriarchy that attempted to protect the women even as it developed a female workforce that worked long hours in harsh conditions. They also found a community that accepted women working in the factories—until unemployment increased or they began to challenge traditional roles.

Two reasons explain women's special place in the rubber factories: tradition and diversity of the product line. Well before B. F. Goodrich came to Akron, women were part of the rubber industry. Census reports show that in 1850, women represented 60.7 percent of all workers in the rubber and elastic goods industry. By the time Goodrich came to town in 1870, that percentage had decreased, although the actual number of women in the rubber factories continued to increase.

The diversity of production in the industry also explained why so many women were employed. The rubber industry produced everything from tires to water bottles, playthings, and sundries. Men did the heavy work, while women specialized in the manufacture of smaller products that required more dexterity than strength. Or as one reporter for the Firestone newspaper reported in 1928, "Women have long since demonstrated their ability to hold their own in certain kinds of industrial work, especially where precision and speed are required. Their nimble fingers are able to perform certain tasks even better than men."

The women also benefited from mechanization. Each new decade seemed to bring new labor-saving machines that allowed women to take over jobs that had earlier been done by men. The trend had been going on for decades, long before the union and long before a writer for the union paper observed, "Operation after operation is being performed by women today in the rubber plants that five or ten years ago was done by boys and men. In many instances men are being replaced by women on jobs for the sole purpose of curtailing labor expense." Those two trends—mechanization and diversification of product line—explained why the number of women increased so greatly in the rubber industry—even if their percentage of the total working force may have declined (Table 1).

Female employment in the factories did not always follow traditional patterns. Before they acquired union representation, some women workers floated into and out of the rubber factory labor force. Some were like Mildred Young, who came in to work for a time before she married and then returned after marrying and having children, or Anna Mae Rhoades, who started at Goodyear in 1913 and still worked there in 1943. During those thirty years, her career saw many interruptions. Anna explained to the reporter of the Goodyear *Wingfoot Clan* during World War II, "I 'retired' two or three times but somehow 'drifted back,' for Goodyear seems just like home to me." Still others followed traditional employment patterns, working on the job consistently until retirement. Lillie Murphy followed that path. She joined Goodyear in 1902; fifteen years later she was a "forelady" in Department 6, overseeing the growing number of women producing inner tubes. Lena Metz started at Goodyear on January 2, 1906, in Department 6. She worked there until 1916, when she transferred to the rubber band department, where she was head in-

Table 1

Employment in the Rubber Industry by Gender

Year	Total number	Men		Women	
		Number	*Percent*	*Number*	*Percent*
1870	3,886	2,035	52.4	1,851	47.6
1880	6,350	4,292	67.6	2,058	32.4
1890	16,162	9,706	60.1	6,456	39.9
1900	21,866	14,492	66.3	7,374	33.7
1910	31,571	21,162	67.0	10,409	33.0
1920	86,177	67,354	78.2	18,823	21.8
1930	80,811	59,535	73.7	21,276	26.3

Sources: Department of Commerce and Labor, Bureau of the Census, *Special Reports: Occupations at the Twelfth Census* (Washington, D.C.: Government Printing Office, 1904), and Alba M. Edwards, *Sixteenth Census of the United States: 1940 Population, Comparative Occupation Statistics for the United States, 1870 to 1940* (Washington, D.C.: Government Printing Office, 1943).

spector for the next five years. In 1921, she transferred to the boot and shoe department, where she was a heel inspector.

Jobs in the rubber factories were seldom easy or the work environment pleasant, especially for the first and second generations of woman rubber workers. One writer for the union newspaper remembered what it was like: "Years ago, women in the rubber plants were compelled to stand all day in many instances to perform their work. Today they are provided with high stools and chairs. Women used to stand in water in some departments years ago. Today, elevated platforms have been erected. Darkened corners have been made brighter by more electric lights, revolving fans have been installed, and conditions as a whole have been improved."

In spite of the working conditions, increasing numbers of women were going to work in the rubber factories of Akron and nationwide. The *Akron Beacon and Republican* in 1895 reported that nationwide more women were employed in industrial jobs than ever before—four million in 1890, up 263 percent from 1880. "These statistics mark the progress of the revolution, so far as woman is concerned," the newspaper commented. The writer also observed that the number of women working in industrial jobs had probably increased between 1890 and 1895.

The writer had only to look around the city of Akron to find proof of that assertion. Women were employed in a range of industrial jobs: as printers, cigar makers—and rubber workers. The numbers were small

Women and children were vital to the operation of the earliest rubber factories of Akron. Row 2 features women workers, and the front row shows the children who worked in the Akron Rubber Works in 1883. *B. F. Goodrich Collection.*

in the late nineteenth century because the industry in Akron itself was just beginning. Nonetheless, at least one Akron minister was disturbed enough by the trend that he devoted four sermons at the Main Street Methodist Episcopal Church in 1896 to the evil of women working in factories. The Reverend J. S. Rutledge asked his congregation, "Who wants his wife or daughter to obey the commands of other men in the shop? When the women go into the shops they lose their social standing. The influence of factory labor may be seen in the fact that it injured them physically." Moreover, factory work struck at the very core of womanhood: "There is not much of the mother left in those who are employed in the factory." Nonetheless, Akron women seemed to prefer industrial employment to housework. The Reverend Rutledge complained, "It is almost impossible to get a good girl in Akron, to do housework."

Notwithstanding these warnings, women continued to work in the rubber factories. New factories—especially those producing bicycle tires, tubes, boots, and shoes—needed them. Newspaper stories regularly reported the opening of new manufacturing facilities in the city. In describing the projected number of workers needed, reporters used ungendered terms. The new factories needed "hands" or "persons," not men and women.

It is unclear exactly what categories of women became rubber workers in these early days. If Akron followed nationwide trends, these women were most commonly native-born whites (although a sizable percentage had been born in other countries) and were between the ages of twenty-one and forty-four. They were probably already living in the city of Akron, because there is no evidence that the fledgling rubber factories advertised out of town for women workers—that would come in the next century. Bertha Callahan and Blanche Shaffer were probably typical of women workers in this early stage. Bertha came to work in Goodyear's bicycle tire department in 1898 and stayed until 1907. Blanche Shaffer had been working at a downtown department store when she heard that Firestone paid well. She was hired there in 1910 and remained

Early women rubber workers often worked in departments with just women. They kept their hair pulled up to keep it out of machinery and wore aprons over their skirts. The only men in some of these departments were supervisors. *Goodyear Collection.*

until at least 1935. The Ohio Census of 1910 reported that 1,495 women were employed in the state's rubber companies (8,779 men were similarly employed). That number increased substantially in 1920, when 3,390 Ohio women were employed in the rubber industry. The largest portion of those women worked in Akron factories: 2,197.

Census numbers fail to reveal the growing militancy among this first generation. In March 1899, twenty-five "girls" of BFG's specialty department walked off the job, demanding more money. They selected one representative to present their grievances to the factory's superintendent. The women got a raise, but their representative was discharged. In a show of solidarity, the other women stayed off the job. Although they were given twenty-four hours to return, none did and all were discharged. The Goodrich superintendent denied that a strike ever took place. "We are simply getting rid of some objectionable characters; there's nothing in the story about the strike," he told a *Beacon* reporter. Women also participated in male-led strikes. In 1899, eighty workers—thirty of them women—walked off the job at the India Rubber Company.

But none of these strikes could compare to the month-long IWW strike in 1913. Triggered in part by Firestone's move to install labor-saving machines and reduce the piecework rate, the strike quickly spread to Goodyear, BFG, Miller, and many of the other smaller rubber shops. At

(*Opposite*) Women were the backbone of heel and shoe production in Akron. This is one department where women often became supervisors. Here women are weighing heels before they are sent to heaters for curing. *Goodyear Collection*.

(*Above*) In the IWW strike of 1913, women not only protested outside the gates of the factories, but they also ran the relief dining room. In the dining room, women production workers worked with the wives of the male production employees preparing meals for the strikers. Thus, the women played a dual role: protester and nurturer. *B. F. Goodrich Collection*.

its height, about fifteen thousand workers were idle. The strike was honored by both genders. Indeed, women were among the most militant, at least according to one newspaper report. Some women wore strike insignia on their clothes; some picketed. The female strikers complained about the harsh working conditions they faced. The *Beacon* reporter paraphrased the women's comments: "They had to lug heavy tires from one place to another themselves, and said that, after two or three years at various kinds of piecework, they were making $1.25 a day. They showed great callous ridges across their hands to prove the roughness of the work."

Women were also among the most effective speakers testifying before the committee sent to investigate conditions that triggered the strike. Women workers complained about the low wages, bad working conditions, long hours, and that at least one foreman who took advantage of his position to elicit sexual favors—all of which was denied by company representatives.

The militancy of these women was not directed just against companies, but also against anybody who threatened their financial well-being. In 1909, when the state legislature threatened to limit the number of hours women could work in factories, the female rubber workers acted. Perhaps encouraged by management, women workers circulated petitions opposing the bill to limit their hours from ten to eight per day. The petition read, "We see no reason by being thus discriminated against nor why, if we choose to work more than eight hours in one day[,] we may not do so." The measure—by implication—would have meant a cut in wages. Many of these women were supporting their families and could ill afford any wage reduction. Women who were working in the rubber factories in Akron were paid an average of $1.29 per day for a 10.5-hour day, the Department of Labor reported in 1909. These wages were considerably higher than those paid women in many other industrial jobs (such as cigar maker), in retail establishments, and in household occupations. But women in the rubber factories were paid considerably less than the men in the industry. The women earned that $1.29 per day primarily through a piece rate, earning money for each part produced, as opposed to wage work that paid by the hour. Under the piecework system, the more productive women earned more; the new workers or less productive women earned less, sometimes considerably less.

Women worked either in departments where men worked as well, as was the case in Goodyear's inner tube room in 1908, when fifty-eight men and ninety-nine women worked, or in departments where few men labored, as was the case in Goodrich's boot and shoe area, according to company records. Women working in departments with men were typically supervised by men. Women working in areas where female workers were primarily employed were often supervised by "foreladies," women who had been with the company for some time. Thus, Lillie Murphy worked several years at Goodyear before becoming forelady of Department 6, where women produced inner tubes; Anna Connor was forelady at Goodrich's boot and shoe department; Rose Yock acted as forelady at BFG's inner tube area.

Working conditions in the rubber factories were not always healthy or sanitary. By 1905, the state's chief factory inspector had received so many complaints that he came to Akron to investigate. Many of those claims dealt with conditions that were specifically prohibited under state protective labor legislation. The law forbade women from working in rooms where dust from buffing machines was present or other dusty work was done. When Thomas P. Kearns, the state's chief factory inspector, came to Akron, however, he found the rubber industry was well within the law. Women were working in rooms with buffing machines, but the dust was not of an "injurious nature." Women polished hard rubber, but that did them no harm. "I find that the work is not of a

The "Zipper Girls" of BFG's Department 25 seemed to take great delight in their work. This photo was made into a postcard and sent to relatives and friends. The women are: (front row) Isabel Nye, Anna Gish, Mary Riel and Esther Swigart; (second row) Lucy Derhummer, "Big" Rose, unknown; (third row) Lydia Korom (now Pastor), Thelma Eaton, Minnie Horn, Margaret Rittig, Anna "last name forgotten." *B. F. Goodrich Collection.*

dangerous or injurious character as stated in the complaints," he concluded. Three years later, however, women rubber workers testifying before an Ohio Senate investigating committee mentioned many unhealthy conditions: they worked with chemicals and solvents that caused rashes, fumes got into their food, they were not allowed to wash their hands during the course of the day, they had to carry heavy pails of benzene, and the ventilation left much to be desired—charges the rubber companies denied.

They could not deny, however, the long hours some women were working. In 1911, when the state factory inspector again returned to the city, she found that at B. F. Goodrich's boot and shoe department women had worked sixty hours one week and fifty the next.

On the positive side, rubber companies could point to innovations designed to benefit women workers. For example, BFG worked with the Young Women's Christian Association (YWCA) to establish a "home" for its women workers. Designed to house women from out of town who were working in BFG's shoe department, the residence "on one of the best streets" in the city was converted to a safe, clean home for the company's "working girls." The home quickly filled to capacity. BFG was also among the first rubber companies to open a dining room for its women workers. In 1900, the company started offering hot coffee to the women who brought their lunches. The *Beacon* reporter explained, "To girls who live so far from the factory they are compelled to carry their lunch with them and eat it cold, a steaming cup of coffee is a great luxury."

Toward the end of this first generation, changes were taking place in rubber employment policies that would alter the characteristics of the woman rubber worker. More rubber companies began recruiting for women workers outside the city. The BFG-YWCA home was not large enough to accommodate all the women recruited with the promise of steady work and high wages. According to the women who wrote to the city's newspapers, the rubber companies were not paying the women well enough for them to afford "decent" housing. The *Akron Times Press* reported, "One thousand girls in Akron factories, brought here by advertisements of rich manufacturers, are living one-room tenement lives in Akron. Their moral and mental welfare is of no concern to the factory owners who are directly responsible for them." The women could afford little more than one room. As "one of the girls" wrote to the newspaper, "I would suggest Mrs. Wright [president of the local YWCA] go and get a job at a rubber shop and see how she would like to work for 10 cents an hour and work 10 hours. And then pay $4 a week for

(*Opposite*) The seated women are trimming heels, and those standing are inspecting heels in an early Goodyear plant in Akron. *Goodyear Collection*.

board in a respectable place." The letter writer continued, "The girl can't pay board, room and washing and clothe herself decently on that amount. We would be the better Christians if we had a little more money to live on."

Complaints did not center just on wages and housing. Some were about conditions in the rubber factories. By 1912, many rubber companies had dining rooms—at least for the women. But these accommodations were not always sanitary. One woman complained that in one company's dining room, "the roaches are so thick that the tables are almost walking." Another woman, Bernice Brown, secretary of the industrial work of the YWCA, said that not enough of the companies had rest rooms, an opinion not necessarily shared by another woman affiliated with the YWCA. Mrs. J. B. Wright, the group's president, admitted that although there were housing problems in the city, the factories provided sanitary conditions, rest rooms, restaurants, and trained nurses. And the YWCA was tending to the women's needs after work with "wholesome recreation" and "educational classes." Mrs. Wright explained, "A thousand have been enrolled in clubs and classes this winter [1911–12], and have been in frequent attendance at socials, song services, etc."

These innovations had not changed the basic nature of the rubber factory or the work in those plants: the first generation of women in the rubber factories worked in an environment segregated by gender. Men held the heavier, better-paying jobs, while women held the lighter jobs that did not pay as well.

The introduction of automobile tire manufacturing in the rubber factories did little to change that basic structure. Automobile tire building, because of its nature, required great strength; therefore, it was defined as a man's job. The first contracts calling for automobile tires did not significantly change the gender distribution in the rubber factories. In 1900, women represented 33.7 percent of the industry's workforce; in 1910, after the rubber companies first got involved in automobile tire production, women's share of the industry workforce was 33 percent.

Between 1910 and 1920, however, automobile tire production increased sharply with proportionate shifts in the gender distribution in the rubber industry. Rubber companies needed more and more tire makers—all men. And though the actual number of women employed in the rubber industry almost doubled between 1910 and 1920, their share of the rubber industry's workforce decreased from 33 percent to 21.8 percent. Women did hold certain lighter jobs associated with the manufacture of automobile tire production, but primary production was done by men. In addition, women retained the jobs that they had traditionally done, especially in the mechanical goods, sundries, toys, boots and shoes, and other lines.

The second generation enjoyed the benefits of modern industrial life—the restrooms, the dining rooms, the better working conditions brought about by the state protective labor legislation that had been opposed so fervently by factory women in the early twentieth century. The new law set the workday at nine hours, or no more than fifty-four hours a week. In addition, employers had to provide seats for women workers, so they did not have to stand as they worked. But the nine-hour day was just the beginning. Rubber companies soon reduced the work-day further. Before World War I, Akron had earned the title of "Ohio's eight-hour town" because the largest rubber companies in the city had adopted the eight-hour day for the entire workforce. As Harvey Firestone, founder of Firestone Tire and Rubber Company, explained, the move was done for industrial—as opposed to humanitarian—reasons, to improve productivity and quality. Firestone observed in a history of that company, "There is nothing sentimental, paternalistic, or philanthropic in our adoption of the eight-hour system. But you can't make men do their best unless you get them fully interested, proud of what they are doing, happier in mind, better in body and spirit, and producing something for the business organization of which they are a part."

World War I was an important event in the story of women rubber workers. Akron's companies got huge contracts for rubber-based war products, and women—more women than ever before—were needed to make those products. In October and November 1918, at the height of war production, women represented 35.4 percent of the rubber industry workforce, according to Labor Department reports. Many of the new women workers, like Mildred Young, assembled gas masks. Others joined the workers producing large balloons for air travel, combat, and surveillance.

World War I also brought the first temporary breakdown between the "men's" and "women's" jobs in Akron's rubber factories. At Firestone alone, women took over the jobs of some five hundred drafted men. Whether they were paid at the same rate is not clear. Rubber companies also eagerly snatched up the female draftsmen trained by the University of Akron. Women were also introduced into other jobs that were redefined as female after the war. In automobile tire production, for example, women took over the jobs in bead making and finishing.

Labor shortages introduced new groups of women into the rubber factories. Some of them made the transition effortlessly. For example, most of the city's teachers joined the rubber industry workforce during

One of the benefits of working at rubber factories was the company store. In 1920, Goodyear sold not only its own products but food as well. Women—both workers and relatives of male employees—frequented these stores. *Goodyear Collection*.

the summer of 1918. But even the suggestion of other groups joining the labor force posed problems—no matter how chronic the labor shortage might be. The rubber companies met with the head of the U.S. Employment Service (USES) in Akron to look into prospects of hiring African Americans in the factories. A committee was formed to prepare a list of African American women available for factory work, but nothing more was reported on the list, the effort, or the issue.

The women brought in during World War I were a diverse group. Besides Akron women, some were immigrants from other countries, like Anna Marie Bankas, who was only sixteen when she was hired by BFG in 1918, and Lizzie Seeper of Yugoslavia, who joined Goodyear's service department in 1918. Others were from small towns or farms in Ohio, like Maggie Simmons, who was hired by Goodyear in 1918 to trim nonskid bands and quickly transferred to stock preparation, and Florence Noe, who joined Goodyear in 1918 to box tubes and then moved to finishing tires. Some were from out of state, like Lula Vowls, who was from Hardy, West Virginia, and joined Goodyear in 1918 repairing flaps in Department 162, and Mary Woodling from Altoona, Pennsylvania, who had attended business college but was hired by Goodyear in 1918 to "lay up" patches in Department 18. During World War I, large numbers of women moved to Akron from southern states to get jobs in the rubber factories.

The influx of new workers brought the city and the rubber companies the same problems—on a smaller scale—that they would face during World War II. Housing, for example, was a real problem because room and board took a major portion of a woman worker's wages. Firestone estimated that a "girl from out of town" could expect to pay $15 rent for her room and an additional $35 for board each month. She also would spend $20 a month on clothing and $8 for "advancement"— or about $78 per month for living costs. There were variations to this

During World War I, more women were needed in Akron's rubber factories to produce war materials. Here women are assembling sections of an airship envelope in June 1917. *Goodyear Collection.*

Assembly of Sections of Envelope

pattern. Some women found homes where they paid only $25 for board. Three "girls" from Akron turned over their whole check to their "widowed mothers," who in turn bought them clothing. Women never needed as much as men to survive, according to Firestone. A single man needed $100 a month for living costs, and a married man, $144.

The companies also had to learn how to keep the women workers on the job and motivated. Firestone opened a recreation camp; Goodyear brought in celebrity speakers. The movie star Lillian Russell talked to women about beauty secrets—the secret of beauty was health; the secret of health was cleanliness. BFG expanded its suggestion program to include women. One of the first women winners was a soldier's wife, Mrs. Charles Himelbaugh, who, the *Beacon* reported, was paid for her suggestion on how to improve the manufacture of gas masks.

These programs were needed because so much of the work was tedious. Many women worked in Goodyear's balloon department, where, notwithstanding the "romance of the airship factory" (as one public relations writer characterized it), the work was tiresome and hard. Many women were required to wear bloomers and work on their hands and knees on the floor to assemble the large balloons. Only women did the inspection—all silk and cotton fabric had to be inspected closely to be sure that all knots were tight. As the public relations writer explained, "So exacting is this inspection that the average amount each girl can cover in eight hours is only 200 yards. This means that the cloth passes before her at the extremely slow rate of only 15 inches per minute."

During the war, company writers always praised women workers. One reporter for the *Firestone Non-Skid*, the company newspaper, proclaimed,

> The bloomer girl is here to stay. She is doing a man's work and doing it very well and when the war is over she will have made a niche for herself in American industry in which she can meet and compete with men on their own plane. The shortage of men during the war will bring about the extensive employment of women in shops and factories and after the war they will remain a big factor in American industry for two reasons: first, women are the equals of men in handling jobs that require quickness and deftness; second, women as a rule, are often more loyal to those they serve and more studious to the little details that go to make perfection in any class of work.

That optimistic prediction never came to pass.

After the war, large numbers of women in all industries were laid off, mostly at the discretion of the companies and individual supervisors. According to the Women's Bureau, the married women were at greater risk and more likely to be laid off. Statistics indicate that this was not the case in the rubber industry. By 1920, more than 25 percent of the female workforce in the rubber industry was married, according to census reports.

Marital status was not the only factor that was considered. Much depended on the job the woman had held during the war. Women who took over men's jobs were transferred back to women's jobs or let go. The women workers did not welcome the layoffs. As one rubber company executive explained, "When the Armistice was signed and the soldiers returned to take their old places[,] the women generally expressed disappointment when they had to give up their positions."

The women who were kept on had been employed in specialized departments. The women in the balloon department, for example, continued because some rubber companies saw a bright future for that product. Other women who held jobs not specifically tied to war production were also kept on. Thus, Maggie Simmons was in stock preparation; Florence Noe was finishing tires; Josephine Rouch was in fabric inspection; Bessie Pitts and Mabel Fridley were in the tube room. Women who held jobs made obsolete by the armistice faced a more uncertain future. Some, like Dove McKain and Ida McFee, were transferred to

Women inspect the balloon cloth before assembly during World War I. Although this was a department where only women worked, the foreman was a man, Rasche or Rausche, the only individual identified in this picture. *Goodyear Collection.*

other departments. More were like Mildred Young, who was simply discharged because production shut down. The gender segmentation of the rubber industry was reimposed, and during the 1920s and 1930s women worked in a segregated environment.

The 1920s promised unparalleled prosperity for the city of Akron, the rubber factories, and the women workers. Goodyear announced plans to build a large dormitory to house between 186 and 190 working girls. But there were problems ahead as the city, the state, and the rubber industry adapted to an industrial slump. The female workers would also face the prospect of an increasingly hostile community that wanted women, especially married women, to give up their factory jobs and return home, thereby easing the unemployment picture for the men.

The crash came in mid-1920. Goodyear suffered the most. Because of an administrative reorganization as well as the post-war economic downturn, Goodyear's factory employment went from 33,000 in early

BFG underwrote a YWCA dormitory specifically so women coming into the city would have a safe, clean place to stay. The dormitory quickly filled to capacity. In this undated picture, women show the camaraderie that they enjoyed at the Y. *Akron YWCA Collection, University of Akron Archives.*

Production could be a dirty job, no matter the gender of the worker. Here a young woman works in inner tube production. All the workers pictured are women, but none is identified. *Goodyear Collection.*

1920 to 7,000 just eight months later. The layoffs were not as severe in most of the other rubber companies. Firestone, for example, went from a payroll of 12,351 at the end of April 1920 to 7,059 in July, according to company reports.

The largest number of those laid off—at least at Goodyear—were men. At Plant One, 23,035 men were employed on January 1, 1920; by the end of the year, only 6,614 (28.7 percent) still held their jobs. In contrast, 1,648 women were employed in January 1920, while only 592 (35.9 percent) remained at the end of the year. The wages also went down. At Goodyear, the minimum wage for women went from $4 per day to $2.40 in 1922. (Men's minimum fell from $6 per day to $4 between 1920 and 1922.) The situation was not peculiar to Goodyear. Across the state, rubber workers were facing high unemployment and reduced wages. Comparatively, however, the women who managed to keep their production jobs in the rubber factories of Akron were paid well. On the average, they earned $17.90 per week, the highest average female wage for any industry and for any city in the state, according to a statewide survey.

The reduced wages and high unemployment of the early 1920s brought forth a loud cry to get women, especially married women, off the production jobs at the rubber factories. One reader, writing in the *Akron Beacon Journal,* urged the women to get out of the factories altogether. They had neither the physical nor mental stamina to do the job. "A woman's wage should either equal a man's or else be made so low that they will go back to the duties they were intended for." J. P. J. provided his perspective to Akron readers: "I am strongly in favor of having the married ones [women] and about 99 per cent of the single flappers also remain at home and attend to their household duties and stop 'scabbing' on the men." In contrast, "Interested" just wanted the married women out. "There is a certain department at one of the rubber shops that has, for some time, made a practice, while work is slack, of retaining its married women, the majority of whom have homes, no children, machines to ride around in and husbands who make good wages. Instead of laying them off, they cut the number of working days to a few each week which makes it hard for the single girls to make ends meet." "Interested" wanted the married women laid off so the single girls could make an "honest living."

Although conditions had improved by 1924, the city's newspapers continued to publish letters from readers who opposed employment of women production workers in the city's rubber factories. In 1927, when the city and the rubber factories had recovered from the economic downturn of 1920, William E. Hampp still complained to the readers of the *Akron Beacon Journal* that married women should stay home and take care of their houses and not "deprive widows, single girls and other needy women from supporting themselves and others dependent on them." P. C. N. wrote on Christmas Eve, 1926: "One thing I wish the businessmen of Akron to do, and that is, to tell the married women now in their employ who have got husbands for them and provide for their needs, to stay at home and look after the household instead of taking some family father's job."

The rubber companies reacted differently to such criticism. Most simply ignored the remarks, but Firestone made it a practice not to hire or employ married women. Women workers quickly found a way around the policy—they simply did not report their change of marital status to personnel and thus retained their jobs. Other rubber companies apparently did not adopt any such restrictions and hired married, single, divorced, and widowed women.

By the second generation, rubber companies began hiring women through distinct female employment offices. For example, at Firestone, the office was run by Helen K. Ebbert, the "Dean of Women." The women hired—like the women who preceded them—came from a variety of backgrounds. Most were native-born whites, yet a sizable minority—almost 27 percent—was foreign born, according to census reports. In Akron, a large number of these women had been born in Eastern

European countries. Alice Florence Banick, a single woman from Bohemia, joined BFG in 1923; Elizabeth Plongar, who had been born in Hungary, went to work at Goodrich in 1924; Rose Hegedus, a Hungarian woman with two young children, joined Goodrich in 1925.

Other women had responded to the labor recruiters who covered nearby southern states during the 1920s. Ida Troutman had come to Akron from Parkersburg, West Virginia, to work for Goodyear; Anna B. Bracken had been born in Birchwood, Tennessee, and also worked for the same rubber company; Ruth Snoberg joined Goodyear just before the crash in 1920—she had been born in Martinsburg, Pennsylvania, according to the company newspaper. This does not mean that Akron women were not getting jobs in the rubber factories during the 1920s. Only Akron residents were considered for jobs when Goodyear began

Rubber factories were not just places to work; they were real communities. In February 1930, women workers were featured in a musical comedy put on at Goodyear. The "Golf form girls" are Vera McClure, Dorothy Carlson, Catherine Gallagher, Enid Cottrell, Catherine Fleming, Ellen Donovan, Dessie Spangler, Pauline Code, and Helen Tennissen. *Goodyear Collection.*

calling workers back after the layoffs. No one from out of town would be hired until all the former employees were brought back, a policy some of the other rubber companies followed, according to newspaper reports.

Issues in the factories themselves also had to be addressed. The rubber industry had long used hazardous chemicals, and many women had complained about them. Until 1923, the complaints had been ignored or denied. Finally, in 1923, the state imposed new rules for women and men engaged in "hazardous work." An investigation into occupational diseases found that 90 percent of the claims came from those employed in the manufacture of rubber goods and from those who used lead in some process of their work. Those disclosures brought specific recommendations: workers involved in hazardous production needed to be examined periodically; workers who had problems with dermatitis should be treated, transferred out of the department, or laid off; workers should be issued gloves for use when handling hazardous materials.

Hazardous materials were only part of the story. Other women were complaining about the general conditions in the rubber factories. One letter writer to the *Akron Beacon Journal* characterized some of the work areas in rubber factories as "places where hogs would hesitate to enter." Another told what it was like to work in the boot and shoe department, where most of the work was done by women: "The boot and shoe department is one of the hardest to work in, and you do not make living wages for about a year, and when you do make it you are laid off to start at 25 cents an hour again." By the end of the 1920s, the rubber companies had recovered from the slump and the number of published complaints had decreased.

From the perspective of pay, Akron women workers had little to complain about. In 1927 Akron industrial workers were paid better than in any other city in the state—and many other cities as well, including Chicago, New York, and Pittsburgh. Employment was up and good times had returned to the city.

That optimistic picture did not last long. The stock market crash of 1929 was followed by the worst depression in the nation's history, a depression that hit Akron and the rubber industry quickly and hard. Between October 1929 and December 1930, Akron factories discharged 14,200 workers, for a 21.5 percent drop in employment. In 1932, only 25,500 were still employed by the city's rubber companies, down from 30,309 in 1930. Layoffs were not necessarily determined by seniority. According to a Labor Department report, layoffs and rehiring in the early Depression period were left to the discretion of management. At Goodyear, "merit" was the first consideration in determining who would

GOODYEAR MECHANICAL GOODS DEPT
SPRINGFIELD LAKE JULY 30TH 1927

be laid off. Seniority was secondary. "Merit being equal, the man with the longer service is to be retained. Merit and service both being equal, then the man with the most dependents is to be retained," Goodyear reported. At Goodrich, layoffs were "pretty much left to the foremen" with a "good deal of weight being given to service." Some rubber companies laid off married women and refused to hire others. Seiberling and Sun Rubber, for example, hired only single women.

Those who remained on the job faced reduced wages, and women were especially hard hit. At BFG, the per-hour average wage for women went from 50.7 cents an hour in 1929 to 39 cents an hour in 1932. The per-hour average wages for men at the same company also went down, from 81.5 cents per hour to 67 cents an hour over the same time period. That meant that in 1929, the women workers at BFG made 62.2 percent of what men made, compared to 58.2 percent in 1932. Average hourly wages did increase. By 1938, the women at BFG made an average hourly wage of 74 cents, while men made $1.12.

The number of hours worked also went down from 42.2 hours per week in 1929 to 29.6 hours in 1933. But the average number of hours worked per week had not yet bottomed out. After recovering somewhat

If you worked in a rubber factory, you were part of the company's "family." Nowhere was that more apparent than at the annual picnics. Even during the Depression, workers at Goodyear's Mechanical Goods Department and their families enjoyed a day at the old Spring Lake Park, July 30, 1930. *Goodyear Collection.*

The YWCA programmed many activities for the women workers in Akron. Clubs and activities revolved around specific rubber companies. These women are not identified, but it is clear that they were from Goodyear and that they were "it." *Akron YWCA Collection.*

in 1935 and 1936, when the average number of hours worked per week at BFG was 32.2 and 33.4 respectively, the average number of hours worked in 1937 and 1938 plummeted to 28.5 and 24.8, respectively, according to company and union records.

Throughout the Depression, women worked fewer hours than men. In BFG's Akron plants, women worked 30.4 hours a week in 1936, 26.0 in 1937, 23.0 in 1938, 28.7 in 1939, and 29.0 in 1940. In contrast, men in the same factories worked an average of 33.4 hours per week in 1936, 28.6 in 1937, 24.4 in 1938, 30.5 in 1939, and 31.6 in 1940.

The situation was not peculiar to BFG. Tressie McGee, who joined Goodyear in 1932, remembered working when her husband had been laid off in 1937. "There was a period of time in there when I only worked two days a week. It turned that slow. I was even working when my husband got laid off," Tressie explained.

Although many men and women were laid off during the Depression, several of the rubber companies continued to hire women for production. Tressie McGee was one of those women. She used her family connections to get hired. Her father had worked at Goodyear since 1928 and had a friend in the employment office. Tressie, just sixteen at the time, was hired; she married ten months later and soon after conceived a child. She worked throughout much of her pregnancy and returned to work when her daughter was only three months old.

During the Depression, Tressie worked in the bicycle tire department. All the workers there were women, she remembered, but "our bosses, our foremen, our supervisors were all men, but the people were—strictly all women." Tressie liked the women she worked with but not the working conditions. "It not only smelled bad, but in the hot weather, ya know—they didn't have such a thing as air conditioning—and those big things where they cured was along the wall where the windows were." She was paid by the piece. "If you wanted to build enough tires to build a day's wages, you didn't have time to fool around." If she was behind at lunchtime, she would "use that time to catch up." Tressie remembered that single women were at an advantage at Goodyear during the Depression. They "could hold a job over the married women. Now that was before the union." After the union came in, everything was done by seniority, she said.

Women were hired during the Depression. Mildred Young returned to Goodyear in 1933 after a fifteen-year hiatus. During that period, she had married and had three sons. When she returned to work, the children

Both women and men lost their jobs and needed work in the depression period. Although most lined up for work here are men, a woman is among those first in line. *Goodyear Collection.*

were young, and she hired a young girl to watch them. During much of the Depression, Mildred worked in the tube room, where women and men worked together.

It is unclear what criteria were followed when rubber companies hired women during the Depression. Tressie used family connections to get in. Mildred's experience helped her. Tressie was sixteen, Mildred thirty-three. Women applying for jobs during the 1930s did not always tell the truth on their applications. Edna Graves was hired on July 26, 1933, but was fired in 1941 for giving false information on her application forms. United Rubber Worker local president George R. Bass explained, "She says girls in the Employment Bureau advised her not to tell that she was born in Canada." She followed their advice. Edna's case was not the only example of deception. Yolanda Bomerato was first hired by BFG in 1935, laid off in November 1937, and rehired in July 1938. When she was rehired, she admitted that she had originally applied under the name and age of her sister Josephine. Yolanda was not yet eighteen when she went into BFG's factory. Dorothy Norman ran into difficulties as well because she used an assumed name when she applied at BFG.

Those situations were probably the exception. Few women had to falsify documents when they applied at the rubber companies. Most simply had family connections. Willa McDonald, for example, got her job with Goodyear in 1930; her husband had been with the company for eight years. Alma Ford followed her sister Lillian Sayles into the factory. The two apparently never worked together. Alma spent much of her time in Department 273A, the hose room, while Lillian worked in Department 162, accessories.

Criticism of women workers—especially married women—escalated during the 1930s. Not a month went by that a letter to the city newspaper did not urge the rubber companies to get rid of all their female married employees. E. M. S. wanted the married women banished from the rubber factories: "Service is all right when it comes to the men. But no widow or single person should be laid off and a married woman kept at work." C. V. H. went even further, declaring that women should get out of the factories altogether. "Ashamed of Our Women" wanted married women to go home and solve the unemployment problem: "I know of a certain department in one of the rubber shops that employs all men, and the majority are married and boast that their wives are working in the same shop." A "Barberton Citizen" thought the best way to get women out of jobs that men should be holding was a tax—two dollars per day on all employers of two or more women. "Help It Along" wanted all married women out, including the ones working under their maiden names so they could keep their jobs. E. M. thought that dismissing the

Mary Ann Arrington, her husband, and her young daughter came to Akron from Texas, Georgia, in 1926. Her husband, O. C., got a job at American Hard Rubber while Mary Ann worked at the old Miller factory and later transferred to B. F. Goodrich. The depression was hard on the Arrington family. At one time, only Mary Ann held a job, after O. C. was laid off. Their daughter Lucrete joined BFG after her graduation from East High School. She worked there from 1938 to 1941. Mary Ann left BFG during World War II. *Collection of Kathleen Endres.*

wives would do a world of good for "the morale of single men and girls."

Thus, even at the depth of the Depression, the women had not been displaced. The women—including some of the married women—stayed in the rubber factories, even as the Depression deepened and as criticism brewed. That was no more evident than in the strikes and union unrest of the late 1930s. Reminiscent of the militancy of the earlier generation, the women were important to the development and growth of the United Rubber Workers. Their involvement can be seen on two levels: on the front lines, picketing and opposing company polices; and, less often, in the union leadership.

The URW was formed in 1935. As more than 20 percent of the rubber-industry labor force, women had a vital stake in the union. During the Goodyear strike in 1936, a few women picketed alongside of men in the "biting sub-zero winds." They shared all the dangers of the strike. At least one woman, Edith O'Hara, thirty-two, of Uniontown, was "shot through her left hand and painfully gassed." She was admitted to City Hospital. Lavada Wilson, eighteen, was not hospitalized but was overcome with tear gas.

Rose Pesotta of the International Ladies Garment Workers Union, who came to Akron as a Congress of Industrial Organizations organizer, remembered vividly the importance of women in winning the Goodyear strike. In her autobiography, she especially recalled the unity among women rubber workers. "From the first day in Akron, I saw that women would play a vital part in the [Goodyear] strike, and perhaps even be a decisive factor in the settlement. True, women workers in the Goodyear factory were comparatively few. . . . But mothers, wives, daughters of the

In the late 1930s, the United Rubber Workers organized the Akron workers, but unionization did not come easily. Akron was torn apart by strikes. Here, on May 27, 1938, bystanders help a woman who had been clubbed during a battle between the police and union sympathizers outside Goodyear's Plant One. *Cleveland Press Collection.*

striking men were there—and we were getting important help, particularly in the commissary, from women employed in the Firestone and Goodrich plants." Tressie McGee peeled potatoes and delivered food and coffee to the picket line. She remembered that the greatest number volunteering in the kitchen were women workers from Goodyear.

Women were also involved in the Firestone strike of 1937. The union's newspaper applauded their role: "Men and women who have stood watch on the picket line all these weeks, all hold their posts, grim and determined, but ready and anxious to start production once more, providing this can be done with honor."

Once the strikes were over, women proved to be effective organizers. They used intimidation, threats, and violence to encourage nonunion women to join the URW. Numerous complaints were brought to the companies about their activity. Katherine Dufford of Goodyear complained to her supervisor about one male union steward who threatened her repeatedly. The union representative warned Katherine that if she did not join, he would have "the union girls in this Department tear her clothes off and beat her black and blue." Fanny Dennison at Goodyear could not stand the pressure from the "union girls" and asked for a transfer. Her supervisor explained that Fanny had reported that union women were asking her to join and the "pressure was more than she could stand." Ethel Ward had experienced the same problem. Union women warned Ethel that if she did not join the union before her next shift, "the union girls would refuse to work with her." The union women did just that to Anna Dominick, a nonunion bead flapper at Goodyear. Anna denied making any anti-union comments but said the women put "so much pressure on her that she hardly knew what she had been saying." All communication broke down in the case of Katherine First and Marie Finney, two third-shift workers in Goodyear's Department 155. They told their shift foreman that as they were leaving the plant, they were surrounded by "union girls" and that "the union girls started attacking them and that a free-for-all occurred." Marie and Katherine charged that the union men kept the Goodyear police at bay during the attack. The shift foreman and night supervisor observed, "Both girls' clothes were badly torn and they showed the marks of having been in a struggle. They were being questioned by an Akron City Detective at the time. The Finney girl was crying so that she could hardly talk but the First girl did not cry much."

Union women, of course, were not the only guilty parties. Male union workers likewise harassed female nonunion workers. Ethel Ward, Fanny Dennison, and Gladys Teter all complained about the high-pressure tactics used by three male union workers. "This continual harassing tended to make these nonunion girls very nervous and their work unpleasant," the shift supervisor reported. Grace Mallis could not continue her work when the "tire builders" stopped work and crowded around her table as a form of intimidation.

Whether because they believed in the union wholeheartedly or because they had been intimidated, women rubber workers did join the union. Some even took places in the leadership of certain locals. Nonetheless, their involvement in the union leadership was limited to only certain positions, most notably that of secretary. In 1936, for example, thirteen women held officer positions in various locals throughout the United States. Of these, four were from Akron or Barberton. Anne Tehensky was elected recording secretary for Local Six; Helen Walker held the same position with Local Eight, as did Lena Fernbecck at Local Twenty and Goldie Rochichaud of Barberton's Local Sixteen. Few women held higher positions. One notable exception was Agnes Kibler, president of Local Fifty-seven, representing Anderson Rubber Company, a small Akron company that manufactured a line of toys, gloves, and sundries.

If the women thought that the union would mean more equitable wages, they were sorely mistaken. The wage differential between the sexes remained. The union did bring benefits to the women workers, perhaps the most important being consistent layoff policies. After URW representation began, layoffs were determined strictly by seniority. Tressie McGee remembered that was a real benefit for married women, who were more likely to be laid off if the decision was left to the discretion of management.

The union also brought in a formal grievance procedure. If women felt that they had been unfairly treated, they could turn to the union. That did not always ensure that they would win their case, but it afforded more protection than they had had before. Julia Propopec, for example, found that the union saved her job in 1939. Julia had worked at BFG since 1933. Between 1935 and 1937 she built up a record of "numerous" short periods of absences. In 1939, she was absent again because of "sickness in the home." Because she had no phone and no access to a phone in the immediate neighborhood, Julia did not notify BFG. She was discharged and not considered for rehire. After the union took her side and presented her case, D. D. Reichow, BFG's manager of industrial relations, agreed to take her back on a six-month probationary basis. The

Although women were often avid supporters of unionization, they were usually excluded from the leadership of the locals. However, a few women—often representing rubber shops where the labor force was primarily female—took visible roles in union leadership, as this picture from the second annual convention of the United Rubber Workers of America attests. *United Rubber Workers of America Collection, University of Akron Archives.*

Mrs. Ellen McKinney, sixty-three, gets a check from J. E. Trainer, vice president in charge of production, for her twenty-five years with Firestone. McKinney was employed in Department 217-A, working on tire plies. She had three children and a son-in-law who worked at Firestone at the time. *Cleveland Press Collection.*

union was also able to get Helen Hilton's "service date" at BFG changed from January 1933 to October 1929. The woman had been carried on the "temporary rolls" for three years; the union asked that she be given credit for those years. BFG agreed. The union also took the part of Arlene Tumlin. She had been laid off February 16, 1939, and recalled on February 24, but she was rejected for being sixty-five pounds overweight. The union pointed out that Arlene had always been heavy and had a good work and attendance record, but Reichow was reluctant to allow her back. She weighed 230 pounds and had been warned about her physical condition in 1936 and 1937. Nonetheless, the union continued to push, even pointing to another female worker who weighed more than Arlene but had been retained because she was the sister-in-law of a supervisor. The grievances, then, covered a wide range of issues: service dates, layoffs and recalls, and health issues. In general, these early grievances did not deal with pay issues or the gender segmentation that remained in the rubber factories.

The union also did not deal with the broader issues that affected women workers. It did not address the child care problems many female rubber workers faced. The child care issue was being addressed by the Workers Progress Administration (WPA) in the city. In 1938, the WPA opened two day nurseries for low-income families—one at the Bryan School and the other at the Allen School. The next year, the Ohio State

Employment Service expanded its child-, invalid-, and aged-care services beyond 5 P.M. to 9 P.M., but those limited services did not adequately address the child care needs of the women rubber workers. The rubber companies did not address these child care issues either, but they were introducing activities designed to appeal specifically to their women workers. Some were sports-based. Women competed in basketball and bowling. Other activities were designed to help women with their traditional tasks at home. In 1920, Goodyear offered a popular "Domestic Science Class." Clubs were also woman-based. The Goodyear Women's Club dated back to 1922.

In 1940, when the rubber companies began war production, they already had a long history of women working in their factories. Patterns of gender segmentation of work were already firmly entrenched. A world war, a new production emphasis, a depression, and a union had not brought permanent changes to that work pattern. Two generations of women workers had adjusted to a segmented work environment in the rubber factories.

These two generations of women rubber workers were going to help with the recruitment and training of a new generation. These experienced women workers would help Rosie in her transition into the factory culture.

The Recruiting & Training of Rosie

Margaret Cooney was twenty-one and had two small children to support when she joined Goodyear Tire and Rubber Company in 1940. She, like so many other women workers, heard about the job opportunities from a relative; her grandfather, who worked at Goodyear, told her about the openings. She had hoped to be hired earlier than her October starting date, but the personnel director, a neighbor who knew Margaret's grandfather, would not allow it. Two things stood in the way: Margaret's age (she wasn't quite twenty-one, at the time the minimum age for working at Goodyear) and her baby's age (her daughter was too young). When Margaret, who was separated from her husband, first applied, the personnel director told her to come back when her baby was three months old. She returned as soon as her daughter reached that age and was quickly hired. That was almost a dream come true. As Margaret explained, "I always thought I'd like to work in the rubber shops." One reason was the money. When she joined Goodyear Rubber and Tire Company, she almost doubled her wages; she went from making twenty-five cents an hour as a sales clerk at O'Neil's, an Akron department store, to forty-eight cents an hour.

When Beulah "Billie" Schott and her cousin Ruth came to Akron in 1942, it was the beginning of a great adventure. Ruth's father, a trucker, had told them that the brand-new Goodyear Aircraft in Akron was hiring, and that sounded good to the young women, who had few job prospects in the small farming community of Caldwell, Ohio. As Billie remembered, the only real job available for young women there was

51

housework—"you worked all day long for $1." Goodyear Aircraft paid considerably more. So the two—both in their early twenties—headed for Akron. They were hired and immediately were sent to school to learn drilling, riveting, countersinking, and bucking. For Billie and Ruth, the job provided a new network of friends. During training, they met Irma Garrett of Stow, Elsie Bucholtz of Massillon, Bea Gillian of Pennsylvania, and Betty Francis of Akron. The six not only trained together, they soon worked and lived together.

In 1942, Grace Hanlon was determined to be hired at Goodyear Tire and Rubber. Patriotism was not the only factor in her decision. "I got laid off from Goodrich and I needed a job real bad," she recalled. When she went to Goodyear, she was carrying on a family tradition. Her mother had worked at Goodyear making heels in the late 1920s and her father still worked there in the pit. One aunt worked in airfoam; two cousins worked for the company as well. With those connections as well as her industrial work experience, Grace should have been hired right away. The woman in charge of hiring females said there was no job available, but Grace would not take no for an answer. "So I went over every day [to the Goodyear personnel office] for two weeks. I took my lunch and I told her that I'm going to bring my lunch and sit here until you hire me. I went over every day. She got sick of looking at me so she finally hired me," Grace remembered.

The experiences of Margaret, Billie, and Grace typified recruitment practices for the wartime Akron rubber industry. First, the family network was crucial. Indeed, this family (and, less important, the friendship) network represented one of the key elements in the recruitment of women. Second, the recruited women often had ties to the rubber industry; relatives or friends already worked in the city's factories. Accordingly, they were familiar with the work and, perhaps more important, the wages offered by the rubber factories. Third, women who joined the rubber industry labor force during World War II were not responding simply to patriotic appeals, even though newspapers and company periodicals emphasized this aspect. Money was an important consideration, perhaps the most important one. These women saw an opportunity to make more money than they had ever earned before. Fourth, wartime recruitment into the rubber factories represented only the opening phase of an industrial career. Wartime work could be the start of long careers in the rubber industry that extended many decades past the end of the war.

The rubber industry was well equipped to recruit and hire large numbers of women. It was not necessarily because the Akron metropolitan area held an untapped reservoir of unemployed or underemployed females. Nor was it because of any especially effective appeals by the rubber companies or the U.S. Employment Service. Instead, the rubber companies could draw on their long experience in hiring and employing women in the factories.

The larger companies—B. F. Goodrich, Goodyear, and Firestone—already had policies, procedures, and personnel in place to assist in the recruitment and hiring of women. For example, these companies already had female personnel directors who were in charge of hiring women for both factory and office. Goodyear had the experienced Charlotte Vollbracht Cook as women's personnel manager. Firestone relied on Helen K. Ebbert. These women assumed full responsibility for interviewing, testing, hiring, and firing female workers at their respective companies. As Elizabeth Manderbach of the Goodyear Tire and Rubber personnel department explained to the reporter of the company's newspaper before the war: "In our department, we're buying service. We must know the nature and requirements of the job—not only of the job today but we must select girls and women capable of moving to a better position. We must select those best qualified to fill each individual position. However, in doing that we must never forget the human side of life." The women who were hired also had to meet minimum physical requirements; they had to be at least five feet two inches tall and weigh 110 pounds or more, according to vocational guides put out by the state at the time.

The exigencies of war, however, forced changes in hiring practices and procedures. The deliberate method of hiring that characterized the prewar period as well as the minimum physical requirements were often set aside as the rubber companies rushed to hire the thousands of women workers they needed to fill defense contracts. Goodyear Tire and Rubber, Firestone, Goodrich, Goodyear Aircraft, and the smaller rubber shops competed with each other for these women workers and also with the other defense plants in Ohio, including those in nearby Cleveland and Ravenna.

From the perspective of J. E. Trainer, Firestone's vice president for production, the best practice was to hire early. In a confidential memo in 1942, he wrote, "By hiring now you can, undoubtedly, obtain a better class of women than you can later on." Effective recruitment was the key. Rubber company executives soon discovered that their best recruiters were their current employees. Family networks in the rubber companies had long existed as one generation introduced the next to the work. The war and the availability of work strengthened the already existing connections.

The family of Anna N. Williams illustrated this system. Anna was called "Mom" by her associates in Department 945 of Goodyear Plant C. She earned her title for a number of reasons. She had been the first woman to join the extrusion milling shop (Department 945), and she was president of the morning section of Goodyear's Moms Club, a group of second-shift mothers who had sons in the service. Anna had three sons and one son-in-law fighting the enemy. She was also Mom because every member of the Williams family except one had worked for Goodyear. During the war, her daughter Dorothy Hykes worked with her mother in Department 945 and another, Regina Hupp, worked in tanks in Plant One. Her daughter-in-law Ruby worked in Department 579 in Plant D.

Frances P. Golliday used her family connections to get started at Goodyear in 1940, when her mother, a Goodyear employee, took her to the labor department, which immediately hired Frances. Of course, she had to falsify her birth certificate first; just ten months shy of twenty-one, Frances changed the year of her birth from 1920 to 1919. Six months later, the employment office called on her to explain. "Somebody squealed on me," Frances said. "So, they [the employment office] confronted me with that." She resorted to tears and was forgiven for that transgression. This was the beginning of Frances's long association with Goodyear. She had hoped to work there for about six months, just long enough to buy some new clothes. But the money was so good—forty-five cents an hour to start—that she couldn't afford to leave.

The family connections were not always through women. Women also followed their fathers into the rubber factories and sometimes into the same type of work. Norma Jean Patrick's father was a welder at Goodyear. She was married to a welder in Ravenna and had learned the trade in a six-week course. Norma Jean was one of the few women welders at Goodyear Aircraft, working on the framework of K-ship cabins.

Thelma Hiter became a third-generation Goodyear worker. Her grandfather R. I. Ford worked in the calendar room, and her father worked in the Plant One tin shop. Thelma also had a female role model in the family. Her stepmother, Naomi, worked in Plant Two braiding. Thelma was hired in the first phase of wartime recruitment. A graduate of Kenmore High School, she was an ideal hire for Goodyear. Not only did she have strong family ties to the company, but she was also an experienced worker, having been employed for two years in a beauty shop. As she explained to a reporter for the company's newspaper, "Working at Goodyear is quite different from working in a beauty shop. It's a novel move for me but I do not consider this a lark. It's serious with me."

In other instances, women brought their sisters into the rubber factories. This was particularly the case for out-of-town recruits. Married

PAPPY HITS UPON AN IDEA

"Mom, you could park the kid with grandma in Barberton or Aunt Sophy in Ellet and take a war job at Goodyear while I tend to the ration coupons."

Although the Goodyear cartoonist was poking fun at one family relationship, the cartoon illustrates several points. First, women were needed and wanted in Akron's rubber factories. Second, women from out of town, presumably the mountains in West Virginia, had a ready-made support network in the Akron area. Third, families were important in the recruitment of women into the factories of the city. *Goodyear Wingfoot Clan, May 19, 1943, Goodyear Collection.*

names often mask family connections. Three Strader sisters, for example, Pauline Strader Taylor, Jerry Strader, and Guinevere Strader came from Weston, West Virginia, to work at Goodyear. Weston was also the hometown for Anna Waldeck, who worked at Goodyear Aircraft, Department 572C, final assembly, Plant D. Anna lived with her older sister, who was married to William Swisher, another Goodyear employee. Anna sent much of her paycheck home to help support her younger brothers and sister. A woman's marital status explained other family connections. Harry Walters worked for twenty-four years at Goodyear before his wife, Elizabeth, joined the company in 1941. Harry was a supervisor in Department 381E, bullet seal tanks, and Elizabeth worked in Department 379, inflatable boats.

This network most frequently benefited white women but could also explain how some African American women were introduced into rubber factories. Before the war, few African Americans worked in rubber factories. The family network appeared to be a factor in the Carrington family's involvement at Goodyear Aircraft. Clarence and his wife, Grace, both worked at Goodyear. Grace, a "member of one of the oldest Negro families in Akron," worked on the assembly line at Goodyear Aircraft (Department 393, preassembly Plant B); Clarence worked in Department 968, Plant C.

The importance of family networks was not lost on the rubber companies. Both Goodyear and Firestone adopted hiring practices that favored spouses and relatives of employees who were in the armed services. That policy brought in new employees like Mrs. William F. George, whose husband had worked in the balloon room, Department 180 in Goodyear's Plant One. She left her twins at home when she took her job making V-belts in Department 271 in Plant Two. She insisted, however, this was just a temporary measure. "When Bill returns and the war is over, I expect to devote myself full time to my home. However, until the Japs and the Germans are defeated it is incumbent upon all of us who can work in war industries to stick to our jobs until victory is done," she promised a reporter for the company's newspaper. Ann Moneypenny, twenty, a mother of a seven-month-old daughter, Judith Ann, took advantage of the same corporate policy. She worked at Goodyear Aircraft's Department 343, Paint Shop, Plant A, the same department where her husband worked before he left for the armed services. To Ann, the job was a natural: "Aircraft was good to my husband. So I thought of Aircraft first when it became necessary that I go to work when Art went to the army," she told the reporter for the company's newspaper.

Corporations attempted to capitalize on networks in other ways. Firestone, for example, posted bulletins at its plants urging employees to have friends or relatives apply. The company also passed out referral cards to employees to distribute to potential applicants.

Unions also played a role. The U.S. Employment Service, the government agency that matched both female and male workers with available jobs, wanted one United Rubber Workers local leader to get his membership to locate even more potential workers. W. D. Westenbarger, manager of the USES in Akron, wrote George Bass, president of Local Five, which represented Goodrich workers, asking him to get local members to locate eligible relatives and friends and have them register with the USES. "We ask your members to urge their wives, daughters, relatives, friends and neighbors to register for war jobs," Westenbarger wrote. The rubber industry especially needed "agile women up to [age] 45."

Friendship networks also worked to the rubber companies' advantage. The friends were not necessarily women or factory workers but included individuals who were aware that certain companies were hiring. For Agnes Lackney, the catalyst was her employer. Agnes had moved to Akron from Byesville, Ohio, in 1937. At the time, she was only able to find a job as a housekeeper/baby-sitter in the home of Dean Sweet, an artist who worked at Firestone. He told her "to go get a job at Firestone," Agnes recalled. She, in turn, informed two friends, all of whom did housework. One Wednesday, the day they all had off, they went to Goodrich to apply. The personnel office there was jammed with people that spring day in 1941 and the three had no luck. So they walked over to Firestone, where at least Agnes would soon get some good news. After a month, she was called in for an interview and was hired.

Judge Clande V. D. Emmons of Akron's Common Pleas Court proved to be the friend in the know for Thelma Moore, who worked as a cashier at the Loew's Theater in Akron. Emmons thought the teen deserved a better job. Thelma agreed but didn't know where to find one. "He [Judge Emmons] said they're going to be hiring down . . . at a new plant down at Goodyear, making planes," Thelma remembered. The judge even gave her the name of a contact. "[He] told me to go and see Whitey. . . . And he called Whitey up and told him I was coming." The interview went well, but Thelma had to admit she was not quite eighteen, then the minimum age for working in a factory. She was told to return on her birthday, three days later, and she would be hired.

Informal recruitment through family and friendship was supplemented by other techniques. For example, the *Akron Beacon Journal* proved to be an important ally for the rubber industry. Through its stories and editorials, the newspaper informed women of the job opportunities and provided the practical information they needed to apply for these jobs. One story assured readers that a birth certificate was not required in the application process and that other forms of identification would be acceptable. Another feature outlined the specific process by which women got defense jobs, even following one woman—Frances Drummond—through the application process and training program. Although many articles did not contain direct appeals to the women, they sometimes had immediate results. A report that Goodyear Aircraft was hiring at a rate of one thousand persons per week "caused an exodus from stores by employees seeking better paying jobs," according to the paper. The *Beacon Journal*'s involvement in recruitment was not limited to its news columns. Editorials also urged women to apply for jobs in war industries. As an editorial writer observed in 1944, "Every woman who is not closely tied to her home by the responsibility of caring for small children ought to ask herself whether she cannot help the war effort in some small way by taking a job."

The U.S. Employment Service and the War Manpower Commission (WMC) used two primary methods to recruit the women of Akron into the defense industries. Advertising in the city's newspapers was commonly used throughout the United States to recruit workers, while a survey method soon became a model for cities across the United States. By early 1942, the U.S. Employment Service was helping to locate and train women workers for the rubber companies. The government agency and the rubber companies concentrated first on finding the needed women workers in Akron because recruiting outside the metropolitan area could be expensive and posed special problems. Defense workers recruited from outside needed housing that was in short supply in Akron. Thus, in 1942 especially, all efforts were focused on finding the needed workers locally. The question was how best to reach this untapped labor reserve.

The first step was to develop a survey that would identify workers. The War Manpower Commission sent volunteers from the U.S. Citizens Service Corps into the community in a house-to-house canvass. The survey was designed to locate women available for employment and identify special problems that kept women from working full time. The survey covered such issues as child care, transportation, welfare, and housing.

Early results identified 7,000 employable women but found that only 1,300 were interested in working in the defense industries. Complaints soon surfaced that this survey involved more than just eliciting information. Akron women complained that the canvassers were using "high pressure" methods to get the women to come to work. In response to the complaints, the director of the War Manpower Commission contacted the phone solicitors who were following up on the survey and told them to "tone down" their high-pressure techniques "so that they would not frighten and anger the women called." Ultimately, after contacting some 51,000 households, volunteers did locate about 11,000 unemployed women. These women represented an informal registration pool, which was subsequently contacted by telephone canvassers. Between 3,600 and 5,000 Akron women were thus recruited immediately into the city's defense industries. The remaining unemployed women were to be resurveyed. In spite of the complaints, the Akron survey method was dubbed a success. The *Akron Beacon Journal* reported, "Akron is farther advanced in employment of women than any other industrial area except the west coast aircraft centers. Its methods and manners thus are lessons for other cities."

The same personal approach was tried the next year, when trained government and rubber factory personnel workers went into the homes to recruit women who had already indicated a willingness to work in a defense industry. As the head of Akron's War Manpower Commission explained, these women would not have "to trudge to an employment office of [sic] stand in line." Instead, the personnel workers would come

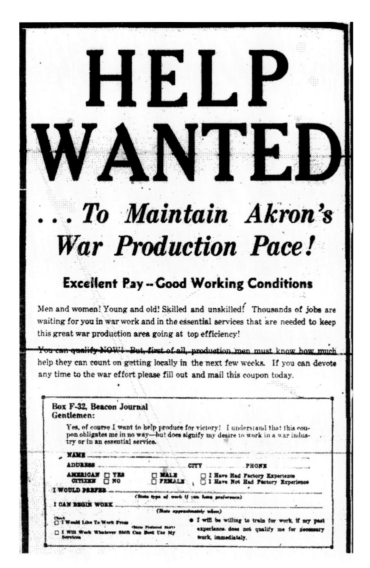

HELP WANTED

... To Maintain Akron's War Production Pace!

Excellent Pay -- Good Working Conditions

Men and women! Young and old! Skilled and unskilled! Thousands of jobs are waiting for you in war work and in the essential services that are needed to keep this great war production area going at top efficiency!

You can qualify NOW! But, first of all, production men must know how much help they can count on getting locally in the next few weeks. If you can devote any time to the war effort please fill out and mail this coupon today.

Box F-32, Beacon Journal
Gentlemen:
Yes, of course I want to help produce for victory! I understand that this coupon obligates me in no way—but does signify my desire to work in a war industry or in an essential service.

NAME
ADDRESS _____ CITY _____ PHONE
AMERICAN ☐ YES   ☐ MALE   ☐ I Have Had Factory Experience
CITIZEN ☐ NO   ☐ FEMALE   ☐ I Have Not Had Factory Experience
I WOULD PREFER
                    (State type of work if you have preference)
I CAN BEGIN WORK
                    (State approximately when)
Check
☐ I Would Like To Work From   ● I will be willing to train for work, if my past
(State Preferred Shift)   experience does not qualify me for necessary
☐ I Will Work Whatever Shift Can Best Use My   work, immediately.
Services

"Help wanted" advertisements during the war took many different forms. Some were bold display ads designed to appeal to both men and women. This ad urged readers to return a coupon to indicate an interest in helping "produce for victory!" However, it did not force the individual: "Please note: You are under no obligation to accept any specific job, just by mailing this coupon. You are, however, contributing a great deal to the knowledge of how much man and woman power is available in the Akron area." Akron Beacon Journal, *November 15, 1942.*

to the women. "They will hire many in their own living rooms," the newspaper reported. Because this campaign was aimed at married women, the personnel worker questioned them about special household problems going to work would cause them. This represented a change in the official policy of the War Manpower Commission. Up until that time, Harry Markle, Akron's WMC director, had urged women with children under the age of fifteen years not even to apply for work unless they had a specific plan for child care. By 1943, Markle rethought that position and actively supported a child care program in the city.

The War Manpower Commission employed more conventional recruitment methods as well. The most obvious were the advertisements placed in the city's newspapers. These advertisements were directed at women and were not soliciting employment for one specific corpora-

1000 WOMEN
WANTED AT ONCE
For Vital War Work!

Akron's war production pace MUST be maintained, and a large share of the burden must be carried by the women of this area.

If you want to do your part to help win the war........if you want interesting work at attractive wages........and with ideal working conditions—

Fill in the coupon below and get it in the mail at once. Akron's industries must know just how many women can be counted on from this area. Let them know—NOW!

Box F-32, Beacon Journal
Gentlemen:

Yes, of course I want to help produce for victory! I understand that this coupon obligates me in no way—but does signify my desire to work in a war industry or in an essential service.

NAME _____

ADDRESS _____ CITY _____ PHONE _____

AMERICAN ☐ YES   ☐ I Have Had Factory Experience
CITIZEN ☐ NO   ☐ AGE   ☐ I Have Not Had Factory Experience

State Education By Checking Number Years Completed

☐ Grade School   ☐ High School   ☐ College

I WOULD PREFER _____
(State type of work if you have preference)

I CAN BEGIN WORK _____
(State approximately when)

Check
☐ I Would Like To Work From _____ (State Preferred Shift)
☐ I Will Work Whatever Shift Can Best Use My Services

● I will be willing to train for work, if my past experience does not qualify me for necessary work, immediately.

Please note: You are under no obligation to accept any specific job, just by mailing this coupon. You are, however, contributing a great deal to the knowledge of how much woman power is available in the Akron area. If you filled in the coupon which was on this page last week—please do NOT mail it in again.

FILL OUT THE COUPON NOW AND MAIL IT TO
BOX F-32, BEACON JOURNAL

Display advertisements could also appeal specifically to the potential woman worker. This one emphasized that yet another thousand women were needed for "vital war work," primarily in the rubber factories. Women were urged to return the coupon. They were even allowed to indicate their shift preferences. Akron Beacon Journal, *November 22, 1942*.

tion. In one early advertising campaign, the emphasis was on locating women and getting them trained. Placement came later. This campaign emphasized patriotic appeals: "IF YOU ARE UNEMPLOYED—OR IF YOU ARE EMPLOYED IN NON-ESSENTIAL ACTIVITIES—IT IS YOUR PATRIOTIC DUTY TO MAKE YOURSELF AVAILABLE FOR VITAL WAR WORK." The high wages received only secondary prominence in those ads. Women were urged to apply for the training offered at flexible, convenient hours. The next month, the advertising directed at women had been redesigned. Not only would women be serving their country but they would also "EARN MORE MONEY THAN YOU HAVE EVER EARNED IN YOUR LIFE." Those types of

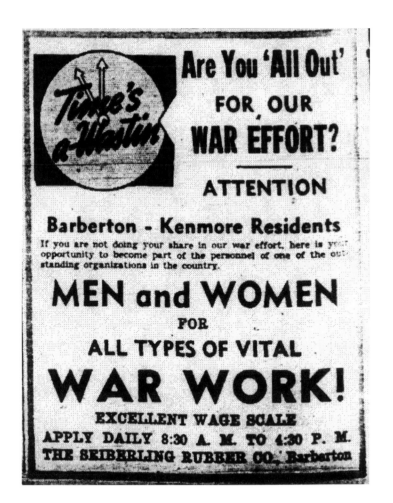

Individual companies ran their own display advertising in the city's newspaper. This one for Seiberling Rubber in Barberton appealed to both genders in Barberton and Kenmore and promised an "EXCELLENT WAGE SCALE." Akron Beacon Journal, *November 22, 1942.*

appeals brought in many applications but fewer than had been solicited during the survey conducted in 1942. In early December 1942, the *Akron Beacon Journal* reported that about fifteen hundred job applications had been received as a result of advertisements.

The War Manpower Commission, through the U.S. Employment Service, initiated other programs designed to recruit women into the city's defense industries. For example, the commission exploited the city's educational system by recruiting girls of seventeen to take training so they could take their places in the rubber factories. During the spring, the WMC appealed to teachers to do their part by working in defense industries during the summer. In other instances, the WMC recruiters went south—to West Virginia, Tennessee, and other states—to recruit women for Akron jobs. These recruits, primarily single women, were guaranteed transportation expenses, living accommodations in Akron, and pay while training.

The U.S. Employment Service also had a key role in recruiting women from groups that had not previously been involved with production

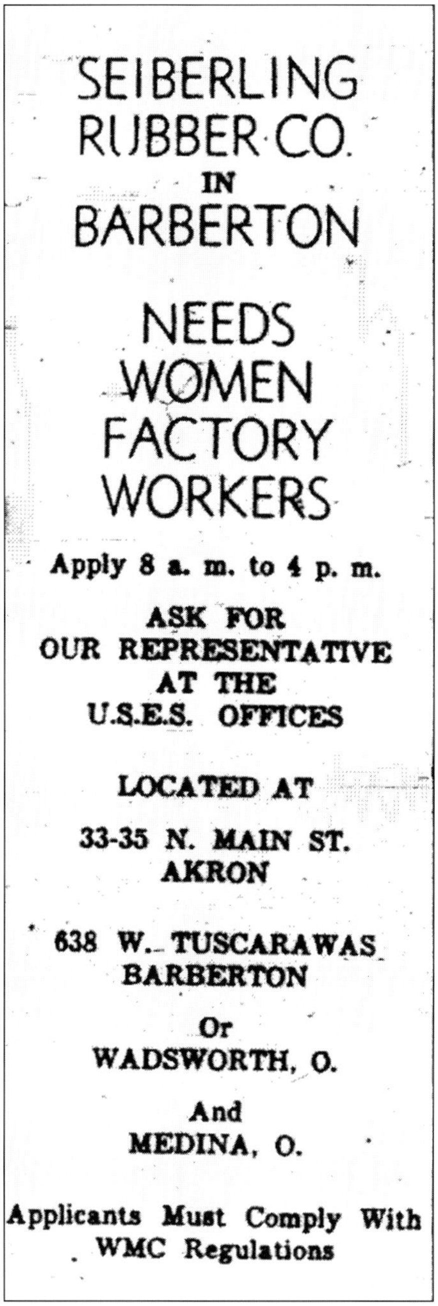

SEIBERLING RUBBER·CO.
IN BARBERTON

NEEDS WOMEN FACTORY WORKERS

Apply 8 a. m. to 4 p. m.

ASK FOR OUR REPRESENTATIVE AT THE U.S.E.S. OFFICES

LOCATED AT

33-35 N. MAIN ST. AKRON

638 W. TUSCARAWAS BARBERTON

Or
WADSWORTH, O.

And
MEDINA, O.

Applicants Must Comply With WMC Regulations

During the war, the *Beacon Journal* continued its gender-specific want-ad sections. Individual rubber companies placed advertising in such sections in the hopes of attracting women to their own personnel offices or to get them to request jobs through the U.S. Employment Service offices. Here the Seiberling Rubber Company urges women to "ASK FOR OUR REPRESENTATIVE AT THE U.S.E.S. OFFICE." Akron Beacon Journal, *April 16, 1943.*

work in the rubber factories. African American women, for example, had held only maintenance jobs in Akron's rubber factories before the war. Because the informal family networks so important in the recruitment of white women were not as well formed in the African American community, the U.S. Employment Service played a special role in the recruitment of this group. Inez Rogers, one of the first black women employed at Goodrich in production, got her job through the USES. Well before the rubber companies began recruiting African American women, the USES sent her to BFG to be interviewed for a production job—and the BFG personnel officer warmly received her. Inez remembered him asking about her family. "So we talked a little bit about whatever and he asked me about the family. I told him I had three girls. And I had three girls, I think, two dogs and a cat. I did. I did. I told him all that. Birds and all that. So he said, yes, you need a job. I said, 'Thank God.'"

Individual rubber companies could conduct their own recruitment campaigns for women in Akron and outside the metropolitan area, but all campaigns outside the city needed the approval of the War Manpower Commission. The family and friendship networks among current employees represented an important and effective recruitment tool. To reinforce this informal approach, the rubber companies used company periodicals to remind current employees of the continuing need for women workers. They emphasized that the company was still hiring and, indeed, desperately needed both male and female workers. For example, in both 1943 and 1944, Goodyear Aircraft used its version of the *Wingfoot Clan*, a company newspaper directed at employees, to publicize that company's labor needs. In 1943, the company needed thirty-five hundred more workers within the next two months. "The war manpower commission believes there is still enough latent manpower and woman power in Akron who can be trained to supply a considerable part of the industry's needs. Skilled men are hard to get, but we believe we can recruit a large number of women who are over 18 and in good physical condition," Harry E. Blythe, vice president and general manager of Goodyear Aircraft, explained. In 1944, the company needed another three thousand workers whom it believed could be found in Akron. In both instances, potential job applicants were urged to contact the U.S. Employment Service and tell them they wanted to work at Goodyear Aircraft.

Individual companies also found that their public relations releases could be a recruitment tool. For example, when Goodyear Aircraft announced plans to hire large numbers of women workers, a flood of applications came in. At other times, companies relied on more traditional recruitment techniques such as classified advertisements in the newspaper. Goodyear Aircraft's advertisement in spring 1943 was typical. "Women of 18 and over who are alert, intelligent and physically fit are needed. If your husband has been inducted or if you have a brother or a son or other near relative, you'll have the satisfaction of knowing that you are helping to provide him with the tools of war he needs." But the copywriter did not ignore either the importance of pleasant working conditions or pay: "Clean, light, brand-new factories, good ventilation, good working conditions, good pay." That "good pay" translated to $33.80

PRODUCE FOR VICTORY AND DEFEAT THE AXIS!

★

The War Production Drive in the Akron plants of The B. F. Goodrich Company has been undertaken by Local No. 5, United Rubber Workers of America, and the Company at the request of the War Production Board.

The purpose of the national movement is to assure greatest possible production of those goods now so urgently needed by our armed forces from Australia to Iceland.

In announcing the nation-wide plan, Donald M. Nelson, chairman of the War Production Board said:

"The War Production Drive is a voluntary effort. Its success is up to the men and women, labor and management in the plants.

"This drive is designed to increase the production of weapons now and not to further the interests of any group. It is not a plan to promote company unions. It is not a device to add to or tear down the power or position of any union. It does not interfere with bargaining machinery where it exists. It is not designed to conform to any plan that contemplates a measure of control of management by labor.

"It does not put management in labor or labor in management. It is not a management plan, a labor plan, or any other plan. It is the War Production Drive plan. It is a perfectly simple, straightforward effort to increase production."

The War Production Drive Committee in B. F. Goodrich is composed of six representatives of Goodrich Local No. 5 and six representatives of the Company.

This central committee, assisted by sub-committees each composed of two members of Local No. 5 and two company representatives, will deal with problems of improved efficiency, increased output, better methods, conservation of materials, and the elimination of waste.

All suggestions from employees will be cleared through the twelve-man central committee and referred to the proper sub-committee for recommendation and action.

Reports on the progress of the Labor-Management Production Drive will be made to the office of Donald M. Nelson of the War Production Board.

A weekly newspaper will be issued for the duration of the production drive at B. F. Goodrich to inform all employees on the various phases of the plant-wide campaign and carry the names of employees whose suggestions are adopted.

★

LABOR-MANAGEMENT COMMITTEE OF THE WAR PRODUCTION DRIVE

FOR LABOR	FOR THE COMPANY
Chas. McCarter	Harry B. Cash
John Saylor	Paul Watt
Frank Payne	Robert Wattleworth
Chas. Corrick	Louis Starkweather
Arthur Dockery*	George Dirks
Thomas Jones	Joseph Hanan*

(*Co-Chairmen)

per week to start and $38 a week after the third week; further increases would be forthcoming as skills increased, and advancement was promised for capable women.

Rubber companies soon discovered that no matter how effective their employees were in recruiting new workers, no matter how many stories outlined the womanpower needs of individual corporations, and no matter how many classified advertisements were placed, the labor pool in the Akron metropolitan area was not large enough to meet the demands. Both the War Manpower Commission and individual rubber companies recruited outside the Akron area. According to the United Rubber Workers, this was a way for a company not only to recruit workers but also to recruit them at lower wages. The union accused Goodyear Aircraft of sending recruiters out to small towns and villages in southern Ohio and offering the women there lower wages than it offered to Akron workers.

Out-of-the-area recruitment increased in 1943, but only after the War Manpower Commission approved advertising and solicitations. The commission weighed labor needs, government contracts, and available housing when it considered whether to allow recruitment outside the immediate area. The companies also had to follow certain government recruitment guidelines. Companies had to pay for the recruit's transportation to the city, and if the prospective worker failed to pass the physical, the company had to pay for that individual's trip back home. Companies also had to locate appropriate housing for these out-of-town recruits.

Recruiters who traveled outside the Akron metropolitan area were almost always men. They went to locations known to have labor surpluses, usually smaller towns in southern Ohio and Pennsylvania or nearby southern states such as West Virginia, Kentucky, and Tennessee. At Goodyear Aircraft, for example, the greatest number of new recruits came from Pennsylvania, followed by Kentucky, West Virginia ("a poor third"), and Indiana, according to one of that company's recruiters. Recruiters went where they stood the greatest likelihood of finding women workers. When a factory closed in a small town in Ohio or a nearby southern state, rubber company recruiters rushed to find workers. They also signed up recruits among the inmates who would soon be released from the Woman's Reformatory at Marysville.

Recruiters looked not only for women (and men) who were physically capable of doing the work (all recruits had to pass a physical) but also were likely to stay on the job. As a result, some recruiters would not separate a mother from her family. As one explained, "I won't take mothers of young children away from their families. . . . I won't separate a man

(*Opposite*) The union and the companies often worked together to recruit workers and keep them on the job producing for maximum efficiency. This insert in the BFG *War Production News* (April 19, 1942) announces the Labor-Management Committee of the War Production Drive, which was mandated to deal with improving efficiency and increasing output. As with most of these committees across Akron and the rubber industry, no women were appointed. *B. F. Goodrich Collection.*

and his wife. They must come together." Purely humanitarian reasons were likely not the major factor. Recruiters wanted women who would stay on the job—mothers who left children or wives separated from their husbands might not stay. Interviewing the woman worker was not always enough. At times, recruiters also met with the parents of the young, unmarried women, assuring them their daughters would be cared for away from home, that they would receive high wages, free transportation, and ideal housing conditions in Akron.

The women who did come to Akron from other areas tended to come in pairs or in groups. In many instances, they came with relatives. In other instances, they were friends or at least acquaintances. The Prosperi sisters from West Virginia are a good example. Virginia and her sister Yolanda came to work for Goodyear Tire and Rubber. The two came with a friend, Blanche Korpinski, who also found a job at Goodyear, and the three lived together.

When recruiters located large numbers of workers in towns, they hired buses to bring them to Akron. When they found smaller numbers, the recruiters merely purchased railroad tickets for them. Once in Akron, the recruits had to pass the physical at the companies, and most did. Those who did not were to be given bus or train tickets back home, but occasionally this did not happen; in summer 1943 two Bluefield, West Virginia, teens were stranded in the city. They had failed their physicals and did not have money to get home. Traveler's Aid eventually helped but not before the case gained much publicity.

Even if the women found jobs, some were simply overwhelmed by the city. The factory work itself did not appear to be the problem; some of the women from small towns could not cope with a city the size of Akron. At least three West Virginia women could not find their way back to the rooming houses to which they had been assigned, and two of them returned to West Virginia soon after. Except for advancing penniless young women money, the rubber companies provided no support in helping with the transition to life in Akron.

Rubber companies also turned to different population groups than had been hired before to find women workers. In 1940, Goodrich hired at least one African American woman for a production job; that experiment proved so successful that the company began hiring more. According to the United Rubber Workers convention proceedings, African American women were working in at least half a dozen Goodrich departments in 1942. Some departments had only one African American woman working, for example, Inez Rogers in BFG's gas mask department in 1940 and 1941. In most instances, the largest number of employees was white, but BFG's workforce did not appear to be racially segregated.

By the end of 1942, other rubber companies were hiring more African American women to remedy the serious female labor shortage. Firestone hired seven African American women but followed a segregated work model. Those seven women were all assigned to the third-shift paint spray booth. In June 1943, J. W. Dean Jr., production manager, wrote to J. E. Trainer, vice president of production, recommending that African American women be integrated into the production process, a recommendation that Firestone followed.

The first African American women hired by a rubber factory were already in the Akron area. Inez Rogers, for example, came to Akron from Macon, Georgia, in 1933. At the time she applied at Goodrich in 1940, she was a widow—her husband had died when he fell in an acid pit at Firestone. As companies began integrating African Americans into production, they were also recruited from outside the Akron area, primarily from the deep South, especially Alabama.

During the war, the rubber companies also hired more physically handicapped women. Unlike many industries, rubber factories had long hired individuals with hearing loss. During the war, the rubber companies committed themselves to hiring more. As J. E. Trainer wrote in 1943, the company needed to start recruiting more African Americans and "more crippled and afflicted persons."

Wartime conditions forced rubber companies to experiment with different work arrangements. Among the best publicized was part-time work. When it was introduced in 1943, the U.S. Employment Service saw part-time work as a way for individuals who already worked full-time to work even more hours. But by 1944, the rubber companies came to see part-time work as a means to bring more married women into the workplace. They could work Monday, Tuesday, and Wednesday or Thursday, Friday, and Saturday. Goodyear Aircraft found this a particularly advantageous arrangement.

The thousands of women who took their places in Akron's rubber companies during World War II attest to the effectiveness of the various recruitment practices. But recruitment practices and policies tell only part of the story. That large numbers of women workers worked in the rubber factories during World War II also represented a conscious decision on the part of the women themselves.

First, financial considerations motivated many—if not most—of these women. The rubber companies paid women workers well, better than the stores and the other factories in the city, a point women emphasized.

Phyllis Douglass went from being a beautician at Polsky's, a downtown department store, to riveter for Firestone because of the wages and the desire to help the war effort. Dorothy Bolen cited the same reason for working at Firestone Steel Products. Financial consideration was not peculiar to one race. Inez Rogers needed the high wages paid at Goodrich to support her three daughters.

Social workers investigating complaints of child neglect emphasized that high wages—rather than patriotism—motivated a large number of married women who worked in the rubber factories. Humane Officer Clarence Blosser explained, "I don't think that any of these women were impelled by the motive of patriotism in going to work in the war factories. . . . In fact, they are all frank to tell me they are going to work because they want the money." Rubber companies and the U.S. Employment Service came to see that and emphasized the high wages in their classified advertising for women production workers.

Second, the women were already experienced workers, familiar with the grind of full-time work. Like the stereotype of Rosie, the women rubber workers tended to be young; published reports varied but most agreed that the average age was under thirty. In 1942, a *Beacon* reporter reckoned that most "feminine laborers" in the rubber factories were twenty-six or twenty-seven years old, although they ran the gamut from eighteen to fifty. A survey of Goodyear workers found that the average age of mothers working at that company was twenty-two and a half.

Unlike the stereotype, the largest portion of the women had previously worked outside the home, though not necessarily in industrial jobs. They held jobs that were traditionally associated with women and not well paid. Some, such as Winifred Petty, gave up jobs in beauty shops to work in the rubber factories. Others were employed in hospitals; Florence Carey worked as a nurse's aide at Akron City Hospital before going to Goodyear Tire and Rubber. Some worked in the sewing trades, such as Juail Frances, who transferred her sewing skills from the Marvin Interior Decorating Company, an Akron firm, to Goodyear's gas mask department. She explained that her eleven years in interior decorating had been an asset at her new job. "I have been able to put into practice all the speed and experience gained in eleven years with the interior decorating concern," Juail said. Others, like Rose Cinocca and Josephine Heacox, worked as clerks in stores before joining the production workforce.

A surprising number, especially among those who were recruited from outside the area, had industrial work experience. For example, Yolanda and Virginia Prosperi and their friend Blanche Korpinski had all worked at the Marx Toy Factory in Glendale, West Virginia, before coming to

Akron. Kay Dallas had worked for the American Viscose Company in Parkersburg, West Virginia. Lana Hudson had worked in textile mills in the South for ten years before moving to Akron. Recruiters for rubber companies were often on the lookout for women who had factory experience. They frequented towns after factories closed down in the hopes of recruiting workers. At other times, they simply went to operating factories without defense contracts to recruit women.

Ohio women also brought in their share of factory know-how. For example, Irene Oliphant had worked at the Hoover plant in North Canton before joining Goodyear. Adeline Getz built plaster forms for fuel cells at the Old King Cole plant in Canton. Dorothy Chevin had worked for General Electric at the Nela Park plant, inspecting light bulbs.

A few of the women, especially those already living in the Akron area, even had rubber factory production experience. Grace Hanlon had worked at both Goodrich and Sun Rubber before starting at Goodyear, and Margaret B. Crock worked for White Rubber and Hoover Rubber in Ravenna before working at Goodyear and Goodrich.

Third, a large number of these women workers had strong female role models, many of whom worked outside the home. Thelma Moore was hired at Goodyear as soon as she turned eighteen in 1942, about a year after her mother had died. Moore's mother had scrubbed floors to support her children. Isabel Moran worked at Firestone during the war, but her mother had been a working woman long before, cleaning houses during the winter months when her husband did not work. When Grace Hanlon went to work at Goodyear, she was part of the second generation of Hanlon women working at the company. Her mother had worked in "heels" in Plant One in the late 1920s. Dolly Bell had only to visit her mother to see a female role model who worked for a rubber company. Her mother, Almeda, came from West Virginia to work at Goodyear, but Dolly found her job at Goodrich. Frances Golliday could never remember a time when her mother did not work at Goodyear. Frances's mother started during World War I. Even Frances's birth did not keep her from work for long; her mother came home at lunchtime to breast-feed her infant daughter. During the Depression, when her mother worked only one day a week at Goodyear, she supplemented her family's income by taking in boarders.

Finally, a sense of adventure figured into the decisions of many women, especially young women. Billie Schott, who came from a small town in Ohio, remembered that sense vividly.

A desire for big wages, female role models, earlier work experience, and a strong sense of adventure did not necessarily guarantee success on the job. The vast majority of the women who came to work in the rubber factories needed to be trained. Training could be formal or informal. The latter occurred on the job. Women learned as they worked, receiving less pay during their training period. In departments where the largest number of employees was female, another woman usually did job training. Thus, experienced women were put in charge of new recruits. Mary E. Thompson, who had been at Goodyear for sixteen years and had built the life raft credited with saving Eddie Rickenbacker, was a trainer in the life-raft department.

When a new product line was introduced, women workers received special training and then taught other women. For example, Dena Johns and Minnie McCoy, "two well-known Goodyear girls," were sent to a government manufacturing operation to learn production techniques in making gas masks. The trainer and the new employee were not always of the same race. Inez Rogers, the first African American woman to work in production at BFG, learned how to assemble gas masks from a white woman and, in turn, taught white women who joined her table. For more technical skills, such as riveting and drilling, draftsmanship, and engineering, women recruits received formal training but seldom came in contact with female instructors.

By far the most comprehensive programs were offered in conjunction with the University of Akron and the University of Cincinnati. These six-month programs, offered with Goodyear Aircraft, trained women to be "junior engineers." Women interested in the program had to be at least eighteen years old and have a strong aptitude for and background in mathematics. The company paid for tuition and room and board; in addition, each woman received fifty dollars a month for expenses. After completing the program, women were given jobs as junior engineers at Goodyear Aircraft.

The abbreviated engineering program had only female students, but the drafting class in 1942, offered through the Goodyear Industrial University, was co-ed. "The girls were carefully selected from more than fifty applicants. All have had at least a high school education and have shown exceptional ability in mathematics, especially in algebra and geometry. Some have had mechanical drawing experience," Goodyear reported. The newspaper called the twelve women in the first class the "experimental dozen" because their success would determine whether it was "practical" to train women in this field. These women apparently demonstrated their capabilities because the training program continued throughout the war. But the age and educational requirements effectively excluded longtime rubber workers.

The classes in riveting, drilling, bucking, and similar skills were taught in several locations throughout the city. The U.S. Employment Service,

(*Opposite*) The University of Akron worked with several rubber companies to train workers during wartime. Two types of classes were offered: the free War Workers' Job Training Program, providing engineering, foremanship, aeronautic, industrial management, and radio classes, and the BFG Institute (four dollars per semester), offering blueprint reading, public speaking, English, rubber manufacturing, and business psychology courses. *B. F. Goodrich Collection.*

ATTEND B. F. GOODRICH-UNIVERSITY OF AKRON INSTITUTE

Study Classes Leading To Certificate
(TUITION)

INSTITUTE CLASSES

Classes begin Monday, September 27, 1943. First semester ends week of December 13, 1943.

General Information — The institute is open to all B. F. Goodrich employees. The purpose of the Institute is to enable B. F. Goodrich people to study or review practical and cultural subjects so that they may enjoy more profitably their leisure hours and secure a better background for their job.

Admission Requirements — The Institute classes are open to all B. F. Goodrich employees. Any questions regarding eligibility to certain classes may be discussed with the Director of Education, located in Bldg. 41-B.

Tuition — The tuition for each subject is $4 per semester if cash payment is made at enrollment or before the first meeting. If payment is made after the first class meeting, a late registration fee of 50 cents per subject will be charged. A semester comprises 12 weekly class meetings of two hours each.

Registration — Registration may be made during the week of September 13, 1943, any day from 8:00 A. M. to 4:45 P. M. at the office of Director of Education, Bldg. 41-B. For your convenience, the Educational Office, Bldg. 41-B, will be open the week of September 27, from 6:30 P. M. to 7:30 P. M. to take care of registration and payments.

Students have the opportunity of taking a course of study with a definite goal ahead of them. They may start a systematic study leading to a Master Certificate. Credit for all subjects taken in the past will be given if they are required as a part of course of study. These courses are designed to cover a period of three years.

Subjects — The following subjects will be scheduled for the first semester of 1943-44:

Blue Print Reading — This subject covers the representation of objects by showing the proper views, three-view drawings, auxiliary view, cross-sections, offset sections and broken out sections, dimensioning, screw-threads, various machine operations and how to specify same on a drawing, section lining, conventional practice, and assembly drawing.

Public Speaking I — The aim of this course is to teach people to outline and prepare speeches and give them in a convincing fashion. It should also teach them to think quickly while on their feet.

Practical English — Teaches correct usage of written and spoken English. Much practical drill in learning to write and speak, effectively. Includes enunciation, pronunciation, grammar, elimination of speech faults, vocabulary development, effective expression and business letters.

Rubber Manufacturing I — A survey of field of Rubber Manufacturing, historical background, crude rubber, plantations, producing tires, mechanicals and footwear, mixing, calendering, reclaiming pigments, accelerators and anti-oxidants, synthetic rubber, vulcanization and testing rubber products. Plant trips will visualize the classroom work.

Business Psychology — The principles of psychology applied to selling, advertising, employment, training, and management; these principles of psychology are given and applied so that the student can apply them in business situations mentioned.

Classes in other subjects will be arranged for any group of 15 or more persons.

War Workers' Job Training Classes
(FREE)

E. S. M. W. T. CLASSES

Our company, through the University of Akron, in cooperation with the U. S. Office of Education, offers the following new courses. No formal academic credits are granted for this work but the University does issue a Certificate of Accomplishment upon completion. There is no tuition fee for these classes. All applicants must be high school graduates or must have the equivalent of a high school education.

Subjects Offered

Engineering

Pre-engineering Math (Shop Math)
Advanced Engineering Math
Applied Engineering Math
Advanced Applied Engineering Math
Engineering Physics I
Engineering Physics II
Tool Engineering
Strength of Materials
Plastics in Engineering
Precision Measurement Instruments

Aeronautics

Aerodynamics
Theory of Compressibility
Engineering Mechanics — Statics
Engineering Lofting
Structure and Stresses
Manufacturing Inspection of Airships and Airplanes
Aircraft Production Engineering

Foremanship

Chemical Engineering for Production Supervision
Elementary Production Supervision
Advanced Production Supervision
Human Problems in Production Supervision
Supervising Women Workers
Industrial Production Problems
Industrial Psychology
Inspection and Testing of Materials
Advanced Inspection and Testing of Materials

Industrial Management

Production Management and Control
Time Study
Motion Study — Work Simplification
Industrial Labor Relations
Personnel Management
Fundamentals of Industrial Safety
Preparation of Manning Table

Radio

Radio Technology I
Radio Technology II

The above classes will be held either at The B. F. Goodrich Company or University of Akron.

Complete description of these courses and information relative to these or other courses may be obtained from REGISTRARS in your division or by dialing phone 202.

REGISTRARS:

A. E. Barkett, Bldg. 1-E
G. R. Shriber, Bldg. 10-D
H. E. Sheary, Bldg. 24-C
C. C. Appleton, Bldg. 24-B

Paul Watt, Bldg. 24-C
H. M. Lacy, Bldg. 25-AA
L. D. Tidball, 426-4 (Mill 4)
C. A. Mears, Bldg. 41-B

You can make sure of getting into these classes by registering at The B. F. Goodrich—September 13-18 inclusive through these registrars.

Girls EARN WHILE YOU LEARN!

Enroll Now for 2-Year Cooperative College Course. Fit Yourself for an Essential Engineering Job in War Production. Work and Study for Degree and Regular Position.

THE COOPERATIVE COURSE

Those qualifying will receive a concentrated program of engineering courses, including mathematics, chemistry, physics, engineering, drawing, English, and coordination. At the same time, students will have a fascinating experience on jobs such as drafting, tool inspection, tool design and engineering estimating. You will earn enough money on the job to pay for your college expenses. At the end of two years, you will be eligible for an Engineering Technician's Certificate and a full-time position.

The course provides for those qualifying— the right to continue for three more years, thus completing the regular five-year cooperative course leading to a degree in engineering.

Early enrollees in this course will be assigned work in May, June, or July to continue until September when college classes begin. At that time, the students will be divided into two sections—one group starting classes September 13 and the other group continuing work until November 1. At the end of the first co-op

period (from 7 to 9 weeks) the two groups change places—Section 1 returning to work and Section 2 beginning classes. These alternating classes continue for the two years of the course.

You are Eligible if . . .

You are a high school graduate, have had algebra and plane geometry, are a citizen of the United States, and can meet the physical requirements.

Sponsored by

GOODYEAR AIRCRAFT CORPORATION

in Cooperation with

THE UNIVERSITY OF CINCINNATI
THE UNIVERSITY OF AKRON

★

If you are Interested — CALL or WRITE:

W. T. CLAYTON, Mgr.   W. S. DOWMAN, Mgr.
Training Division   *or*   *Salary Personnel Dept.*
GOODYEAR AIRCRAFT CORP.   GOODYEAR AIRCRAFT CORP.
Akron, Ohio   Akron, Ohio
Telephone: FR-1471, Ext. 449   Telephone: FR-1471, Ext. 214

N. P. Clark, Goodyear Industrial University instructor, outlines drafting concepts to two unidentified women, who were taking a three-month training course to be "junior" draftsmen. *Goodyear Collection*.

the aircraft industry, and the city's board of education sponsored two facilities. The schools were designed primarily to teach prospective employees of the aircraft industry that, in Akron, was run by the rubber companies. The schools, which were run on four six-hour shifts for three to four weeks, were free and taught such skills as sheet metal fabrication, layout, drilling, metal forming, subassembly, riveting, and template making. But in 1942, the schools operated at less than 25 percent capacity.

The training schools run by the individual companies appear to have been the more popular option. The largest number of the women applied directly to Goodyear Aircraft and were immediately placed in the company's training program. Billie and Ruth Schott, cousins from Caldwell, Ohio, not only learned the skills needed to work at the plant but also earned money and met a new group of friends.

Although the women learned their skills well, advanced technical training for women was always seen by the rubber companies as a temporary

(*Opposite*) Goodyear Aircraft, in cooperation with the University of Cincinnati and the University of Akron, offered factory "girls" a "concentrated program of engineering courses," leading to an Engineering Technician's Certificate and a full-time job—and even to a college degree in engineering. *Collection of Kathleen Endres*.

measure, designed to meet the exigencies of war. Regular apprenticeship programs continued to be restricted to men, which illustrated the rubber companies' intent to retain their gender-based, two-tier work system after the war.

four

Rosie at Work

Frances Golliday's first job at Goodyear was making barrage balloons. It was January 1941, and the nation was not yet at war. Nonetheless, Goodyear and the rest of the rubber companies were already in the war-production business. Balloon assembly took place on two levels—on the tables and on the floor, the latter by far the harder of the two jobs. Frances remembered wearing "big yellow bloomers, one size fits all, and you had these moccasins and the toes turned up on you." She and the other women on the floor had to put the balloon panels together. "You had to roll them with a roller. And when they were put together, you went inside this big envelope, they called it. You'd get drunk in there—from the fumes." Women who went inside to double-check the seams came out "with a pretty good high on," Frances recalled.

Frances did not stay long in barrage balloons. She went on to deicers, working with men. "I was just a young kid. They were older men and, of course, they teased me and told me all kinds of stories and jokes and dirty jokes and stuff like that. [They] tried to embarrass me—is what they tried to do. But they were very nice," Frances explained. She didn't stay long in deicers either. Soon she was in gas masks. By then married, Frances, now Olechnowicz, became supervisor of that all-female department. Her department was racially integrated, and she never noticed any racial tensions on the job or in the lunchroom. Frances liked being a supervisor and remained on that job until the end of the war, when she returned to production work.

Meanwhile, Thelma Bolen was working at Goodyear Aircraft. She was eighteen when she started working at cold, drafty Plant D in 1942. She did a variety of jobs on the Corsairs: wiring, riveting, drilling. Her job took an enormous amount of physical dexterity and agility—she crawled around inside the frames and scampered up and down ladders to get to the instrument panels she had to wire and the places she needed to drill and rivet. Eventually, Thelma got a job helping a man who stretched cables on a machine. When he was drafted, she took his place—after she demonstrated she could lift rolls of cable onto the machine. It was a "man's job" and she was supposed to be paid accordingly, but Thelma had to file a grievance to get the extra wages. She remembered, "They [Goodyear Aircraft] weren't giving me any more money than what I was making so I thought that wasn't right because I knew what he had made, and so . . . I went and asked them [the union] about it and they said, 'Yes. You'll get the same pay the man was getting. You're doing the job of a man's work.' So that made me feel better." Still Thelma wasn't happy at Goodyear. She hated the hours on the first shift—6 A.M. to 2 P.M. Thelma complained, "I didn't like to have to stand on the corner—we had to share the ride . . . [and] it was a hardship to where we parked. We had to walk across tracks to go to the entrance to where we went in. . . . It was there in the area with the tracks, I slipped on them and I fell and I messed my elbow up."

Shortly after, Thelma went to Firestone to work, again on planes. She worked second shift (2 P.M. to 10 P.M.) and liked the hours better. Transportation was no real problem, although the buses were always crowded. The problem was the people in her department. Thelma thought the women seemed just too "lovey-dovey" with the men. So she kept to herself and worked on her job in inspection. When she became pregnant, Thelma did not tell anyone at Firestone, but the company doctors found out after she passed out while she was inspecting the tail section of a big transport plane. Once the doctor discovered her pregnancy, she was not allowed back on her old job. The doctor wanted her inspecting only in the smaller areas. Thelma did not want to do that so she took a leave of absence but never returned to work in any rubber factory again.

Before going to work at BFG, Inez Rogers did housekeeping, but she made the transition into production work effortlessly. She started in gas masks. "Everybody there was white, except me," Inez recalled. "Of course, me, I talk to anybody and make friendships and things like that." Factory production took some time to learn. "I made more money doing housework than I did at Goodrich when I first got started," she remembered of the piecework. Once she learned the job, everything went fine. She got so good at the work that she taught others—white women—how to do the job.

Inez developed a close circle of friends in that department. She and three white women were "just like sisters," she recalled. The four worked together, ate together, and had good times off the job as well. It was this camaraderie that one Goodrich guard found so objectionable. One guard "tried to get nasty," Inez explained. "But I said, 'I'll pray for you.' I guess he didn't like to see us together."

One day, Inez and her friends were called to the personnel office. The personnel officer wanted to transfer all four to Miller Rubber. The four agreed, but the personnel officer cautioned the white women that they would need to look out for Inez because there had only been one other African American woman working at Miller and she had worked in maintenance.

At Miller, Inez and her three friends were assigned to inspection. She had real problems at Miller, but it was not the work or the companionship. It was the heat. The oven blasted, and Inez simply could not adjust to the high temperatures. She worked over by the windows, but nothing seemed to help. "I sure did hate it but I had to leave," Inez explained. In 1944, she quit Goodrich, but she had not given up on working for rubber companies. She went to the employment office to find a new job, hoping for one at Goodyear. But she could not afford to wait to be called. Instead, she went back to housework temporarily. This "temporary" job turned into years of work. Inez kept her Goodrich friends for a while, but over the years she lost track of them. As these three women illustrate, Rosie the Rubber Worker did not face a single experience in the rubber factories of Akron—the experiences were as varied as the women themselves.

Diversified and increased war production, labor shortages, and the military draft worked in the favor of women—at least temporarily—improving their situation in the rubber factories. Throughout the war, women increased their share of the production workforce as well as their actual numbers. The proportion of women went from 24.6 percent of all the production rubber workers in October 1939 to 37.4 percent in 1943 (see Table 2).

The yearly averages mask variations in employment. In 1943, although the average number of women employed was 72,600, the real numbers were higher. Between May and June 1943, employment of women in production went from 69,900 to 72,000, and the numbers continued to increase until March 1944, when 77,600 women were employed in production in the rubber industry. After that, the numbers declined.

Corporate and union archives suggest how greatly rubber companies

Table 2

Estimated Number of Production Rubber Workers by Gender

(in thousands)

Date	Total number	Men		Women	
		Number	*Percent*	*Number*	*Percent*
October 1939	134	101.0	75.4	33.0	24.6
October 1940	133	99.2	74.6	33.8	25.4
April 1941	151	109.0	72.2	42.0	27.8
October 1941	163	117.6	72.L	45.4	27.9
April 1942	141	101.4	71.9	39.6	28.1
October 1942	168	107.2	63.8	60.8	36.2
1943 average	194	121.3	62.6	72.6	37.4
1944 average	204	129.6	63.7	74.1	36.3
1945 average	196	135.2	69.1	60.6	30.9
1946 average	216	164.0	75.7	52.4	24.3

Source: Department of Labor, Bureau of Labor Statistics, *Handbook of Labor Statistics*, Bulletin 916, 147th ed. (Washington, D.C.: Government Printing Office, 1948).

relied on women to meet their production requirements. Firestone increased its employment of women by more than 450 percent during the war. Goodyear and Goodrich also had more women employees than ever before. In 1943, Goodyear Tire and Rubber employed almost 6,000 women. In June 1944, BFG peaked with 6,500 women workers in production. When a *Beacon Journal* reporter wrote about "an industrial world of women, tucked away in the vast recesses of Ohio's largest recreational building . . . turning out defense items ranging from life belts to barrage balloons at record speeds," he could as easily have been speaking about BFG and Firestone as Goodyear.

These women made everything from gas masks to barrage balloons, from deicers to bullet-resisting gas tanks, from bicycle tires to car tires. When the rubber industry added airplane production to its rapidly expanding product base, that diversification quickly increased women's employment opportunities. At Firestone Aviation Products and Goodyear Aircraft, large numbers of women worked to manufacture Corsairs, FG-1 fighter planes, B-26 and B-29 parts, and other aircraft.

At Firestone Aviation Products, women represented more than 50 percent of the production labor force. One estimate put the number of women workers at Goodyear Aircraft at 60 to 70 percent of the total workforce. By November 1943, Goodyear Aircraft was the largest employer of women in the city of Akron. The large numbers of women workers made Akron a hub of female employment during World War II, second only to Cleveland in the number of women workers in Ohio. In 1943, Akron had thirty-five thousand women workers, compared to Cleveland's forty-one thousand.

The first major surge of wartime hiring of women occurred in 1940. At this point, government contracts were for products commonly associated with the rubber industry: balloons, gas masks, life jackets. Later contracts called for new products designed to wage a modern war: bullet-resisting fuel tanks, oxygen cylinders, anti-aircraft gun mounts, and carriages. Again, the rubber industry tapped women workers. At Firestone, women did all the wiring for the Bofors gun mounts and carriages and accounted for about 38 percent of the workforce producing the bullet-resisting fuel tanks.

In January 1941, women were already working in special departments in Goodyear. Pictured are women making gas masks for the U.S. Army. *Cleveland Press Collection*.

Gearing up for war production presented a problem. Since the country had been at peace for two decades, the rubber companies had cut back considerably on the manufacture of products that could be used in wartime. For example, Goodyear had cut its balloon/blimp production to a skeleton workforce of about sixty. When war seemed inevitable, this crew had to be expanded quickly. The greatest number of new hires were women. It seemed natural—production of barrage, sausage, and observation balloons was nothing more than dressmaking on a grander scale, the public relations releases and news stories emphasized. One reporter for the *Beacon Journal* explained that this production was "strictly women's work. Women cut out the pieces . . . long stripes of rubber impregnated fabrics, like so many stripes of cloth to go into a dress. They lay them out on the big floor and cement and tape the seams and in no time they've got a balloon ready." This report was typical. Rubber industry executives, public relations writers, and newspaper reporters

Bofors guns were important armaments during World War II. Both women and men at Firestone were involved in their production. *Firestone Collection, University of Akron Archives.*

frequently equated factory production with jobs traditionally associated with women in the household. As one early Firestone memo noted, "Because the job is primarily one of assembling fabric, women have been found to be especially suited for this type of work."

Women making life vests were nothing more than seamstresses—on the production line. According to a Goodyear news release, making inflatable life vests for pilots "proved another 'natural' for seamstresses." Much the same could be said for gas mask production. "Most of the building and assembly operations in the production of gas masks also proved admirably adapted to the 'feminine touch.'"

That analogy could not stand up under close scrutiny. Making barrage, observation, and sausage balloons, life vests, and gas masks was tedious and taxing work, notwithstanding the public relations releases and the news stories. One reporter for an out-of-town paper removed much of the image of femininity associated with such jobs. In Firestone's

Barrage balloon production at BFG took place on many levels, and women did almost all the work. This photo illustrates the grueling work done by women who worked all day on their hands and knees on the floor assembling the huge envelopes and those who are putting the finishing touches on the already inflated balloons. *B. F. Goodrich Collection.*

An unidentified woman at BFG works assembling a life vest. Uniforms were not required for women production workers, although they were available—at the worker's expense. *B. F. Goodrich Collection.*

balloon production area, "Hands and fingers calloused and worn, feet encased in moccasins or soft slippers (they mustn't tread rough-shod on the paper-thin fabric), these women piece together strip by strip in a tedious, never-ending routine, the billowing monsters which are the bane and menace of dive-bombing pilots."

Women who worked on the tables faced the endless monotony of putting the rubberized pieces of fabric together and cementing them in place. The seams were dusted with soapstone, Margaret Cooney recalled, and that step in production caused her no end of problems. She stayed in the department for eight months but was forced to transfer out when the rashes on her arms would not go away. Her doctor said she had sensitive skin that was reacting to the chemicals she used in production.

The jobs on the floor posed different risks. Women worked on their hands and knees, assembling the "billowing monsters." Frances Golliday remembered the work as a "tough job." She and all the other women working on the floor had to wear uniforms—"big yellow bloomers" and moccasins. The women took the fabric that had been cemented by the workers on the table and assembled them. And when they were done, the women workers had to go into the balloons to check their work. Frances remembered the smells and the strange sensations inside the envelope; she equated it to a "pretty good high." Cecelia (Sally) Foore, who worked at Goodyear, recalled the feeling vividly: "They partially blew it [the balloon] up with air. Sometimes the air was caustic and dangerous. Sometimes we were partially drunk from the fumes. We acted that way as our heads were spinning, and it was difficult sometimes to walk straight. We had two ten-minute breaks for a smoke and a twenty-minute break for lunch and smokes. I didn't smoke, but usually took the break to come back to earth." In spite of these sensations, Sally stayed in the balloon room. She didn't want to give up the friends she made there. Frances and Margaret did not feel as close an attachment to the department. Margaret transferred out for health reasons; Frances looked for more money and a job where she wasn't on her hands and knees all day.

The largest number of the workers in the balloon department, an estimated 80 percent at Firestone, were women. BFG and Goodyear followed a similar employment pattern. Margaret Cooney remembered that the women in her department were mostly young women from outside the Akron area—West Virginia and Kentucky primarily. Sally wrote that most of the women she worked with in the balloon room were married—and most had children. "We didn't talk much inside the balloon, but made up for lost time in the smoking booths. Usually we talked about family, our kids." She remembered, "We all had children, except a few women."

After Margaret transferred out of the balloon room, she worked in gas mask production. Production was broken down into its component parts—all done by women. Some, like Margaret, sewed the harnesses; others assembled the eye pieces; a few did the inspection; fewer were supervisors. This department was a distinctly female environment—but an environment that precluded much interaction, except at break time or at lunch. She remembered that the sewing machines were lined up with one set of women doing that job and another working on tables assembling the gas masks.

Inez Rogers explained that assemblers "had to work fast because it was piecework." The piecework pay rate meant that there was little time for conversation.

It was in this department that Frances Olechnowicz got her first opportunity to be a supervisor. It was 1944, and Frances seemed to be an ideal candidate for such a position. She had been with the company for three years, had worked in a variety of jobs, and had a good work record.

Apparently, she had no problems with the job. The women who worked making gas masks accepted her as supervisor just as easily as they had accepted earlier changes. At Goodyear by 1944, the gas mask department was integrated and Frances reported no problems.

World War II brought a redefinition of "women's work." A "job analysis" by the rubber companies found that women could handle the manufacture of such products as bullet-resisting fuel tanks. Although that work had little to do with the traditional jobs women did in the home, many news releases and features and stories nonetheless tried to make a connection. In one story, a reporter compared a combat airplane fuel tank with a dressmaker's form: "In a technique reminiscent of a dressmaker forming a garment on a dressmaker's dummy, Miss Betty Weinberg applies the initial ply on a form as the first step in making the sealing member of a combat airplane fuel tank. Considerable adeptness and skill in piecing and splicing the material is required for when completed the sealing member must make the fuel tank bullet-sealing to

At Goodyear, rows and rows of women worked on sewing machines making life vests for aviators. The arrangement of sewing machines prevented much interaction among women during the shift. *Goodyear Collection*.

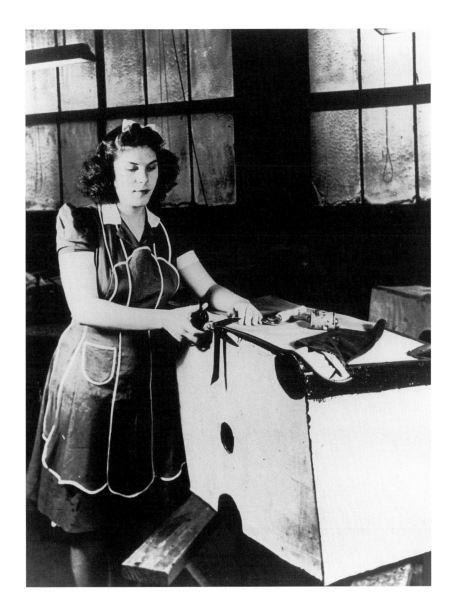

The rubber companies liked to emphasize the connection between the jobs women did in the factories and their traditional duties in the home. *B. F. Goodrich Collection*.

prevent the leakage of fuel even though the tank is punctured many times by high caliber machine gun bullets. Miss Weinberg is employed at The B. F. Goodrich Company, Akron, Ohio."

No dressmaker's form was ever as large as the airplane fuel tank; no dressmaker shop was ever as dirty as the factory; no dressmaker's job was ever as arduous. Tressie McGee remembered what it was like to work on those large fuel tanks. Women applying the rubber plies to the fuel tank always worked in pairs. It was a dirty job, one that required workers to use chemicals when making the rubber fabric connections. Tressie guessed that the chemical was benzene. Those chemicals as well as the dirty conditions in the factory were causing all kinds of physical problems for Tressie. She had a leg injury that was not healing. Finally, the doctor gave her an ultimatum: leave the rubber shop or risk losing her leg. She left the rubber company shortly thereafter.

Margaret Cooney worked in fuel tanks as well but had a more positive experience. Her partner was her best friend, Dorothy Rightmyer. She and Dorothy worked on the large fuel tanks, which required the two to climb up on scaffolds. The job wasn't easy, but Margaret recalled that at least they could talk while they worked.

Of all things about this department, Betty Lange remembered the odor. She and her mother were working at Seiberling Rubber making fuel tanks in the summer of 1944. "The gas tanks were oddly shaped wooden shells which we covered with many different layers of fabric produced by the Seiberling Company. The strong adhesive smell remains unforgettable," she recalled.

After the gas mask department closed, Margaret Cooney had to go to the bicycle tire room. It was the night shift and it was a filthy job. Margaret remembered what she was required to do: "You had to grab them

War production jobs could be dirty business as this photo from Goodyear demonstrates. *Goodyear Collection.*

[bicycle tires] off the conveyor, put them on the table, get a knife. Then you had to turn this table and I had a real problem with my wrist because you had to turn the table and use this hand to clean them with. They called them [the excess rubber] tits and [you had to] get all them off . . . then you'd take a sponge and dip it into this lampblack and clean it. Dirty, dirty job. You looked like, I don't know what, when you go out because no matter how much you cleaned them, you still splattered that lampblack and it was wet and it would be all over you." When that was done, Margaret had to throw the tire back onto the line. It was endless, difficult work. She couldn't afford to interrupt her pace because she was paid on a piece rate.

Here men and women work together at Goodyear to make bullet-sealing gas tanks used in airplanes. *Goodyear Collection.*

Other jobs were easier and much more appealing—even if they were piecework. Agnes Lackney remembered one of those jobs at Firestone's Steel Products plant. Her first job was seam welding, "but I didn't like it, so I got on the pickle tank," she recalled. In seam welding, women had to pick up oxygen tanks, put them on a machine, and weld them. It was hard, heavy work. When Agnes saw her chance, she transferred over to the pickle tank, where the work was much easier. She had only to hang oxygen tanks on hooks when they got out of the anodizing tank, the pickle tank. The job wasn't hard and she and her workmates could talk as they did their work.

That kind of camaraderie was also present in the new aviation assembly plants. Goodyear Aircraft, the largest employer of women in the city, did not have a long history of employing women—it did not have a long history of employing anyone. The company was not incorporated until 1939. Nonetheless, its timing was propitious. Goodyear Aircraft started business about the same time the government was about to let contracts. The only problem was hiring enough men—and especially women—to fill its production quotas. In hindsight, Goodyear Aircraft probably should never have been located in Akron. At least that was the feeling of the head of Akron's War Manpower Commission, Harry Markle: "Whereas most cities had to be sold on the idea of using women in industry for war work, Akron had used them for production and, thus, did not have as large an untapped supply of women power available when hiring for war industry here began." About half of the workers building Corsairs and parts and surfaces for bomber and fighter planes at Goodyear Aircraft were women. In 1943, when the company was at peak production, according to company reports, 31,877 were employed at Goodyear Aircraft. Women learned the riveting, bucking, and drilling skills in training schools. Most women remained with their classmates when they started production work.

Beulah "Billie" Schott went straight from the training school to work on the Corsairs at Goodyear Aircraft. Her friends from training were in the same department, and her job was exactly what she had learned in the Goodyear training program: drilling, riveting, countersinking. It was a noisy job, and there wasn't much time for socializing. Billie explained, "I liked it [her job] real well. People were nice and bosses were real nice men. They treated us nice. We all seemed to like it. No one ever complained about wanting to quit. And I'm sure we got paid good." Happy with what she did, in a department with her friends, Billie didn't transfer around at Goodyear Aircraft. In fact, that seemed to be one of the things that set the aircraft areas apart from the rubber production plants. Women in aircraft production did not move around much.

Dorothy Chevin was a sprayer and dauber on P-38s, in the paint department. She had to pry two parts of the wing apart and spray inside. Dorothy remembered only one transfer. One day, she tried to work in the "dope" room, where Goodyear was having trouble finding workers. She spent the whole day there even though the odor made her sick. "I stuck out the day but I told them no more," she explained. "The higher wage was the thing that drew them [workers in the dope room]. It seems to me it was almost double what the rest of us was making but I said it wasn't worth it to me to be sick to my stomach. I suppose in time you could get used to it but I'd just be curious to know how many of those people are still alive."

Dorothy was issued a range of protective gear, most of which she left in her locker. She did wear her safety goggles—"most of the time because the spray paint could get in your eyes"—and the heavy rubber apron. She didn't wear the mask—and supervisors tended to look the

Martina Bonner (left) and Marjorie Parker are shown riveting a wing for a bomber at Goodyear Aircraft in 1942. *Cleveland Press Collection.*

other way about it. Dorothy was injured once when she was on the job—when she wasn't wearing her safety goggles. She remembered that her brush slipped and went right into her eye. She was rushed to the dispensary, where the nurse tended to her injury and sent her home.

Mary Wagner was wearing her protective cap when she was hurt. She and her partner were working on the underside of a B-26 bulkhead when the drill slipped. Before she could shut it off, the bit hit her forehead and twisted around a few strands of hair that had worked their way out from under her cap. The bit ripped the hair out. Her workmates took her to the dispensary for first aid. It was only a minor friction burn, the nurse said. But later at home, "when I took the pins out of my hair to brush it, I discovered that a large two-inch side section right in front was only being held in by the hair pins. All the hair came out when I brushed it," she remembered. Mary soon became an exhibit. Her boss took her to all the departments to show what carelessness could lead to.

In February 1944, Goodyear Aircraft produced its thousandth Corsair. The plane was decorated with appropriate captions: "THE FIRST 1000 is the TOUGHEST but it makes Poor TOJO's way the ROUGHEST," "KNOCK BEFORE ENTERING," "LOOK OUT TOJO YOU UGLY BOZO." The caricature is of General Hideki Tojo. *Goodyear Collection.*

Women at Firestone's Aviation Products had their share of accidents. For example, Isabel Moran did wiring on planes. In the process, she had to go up and down ladders. "That one ladder we had to use was really high 'cause those planes were big. They were cargo planes." One day she missed a step and fell, landing on the cement floor. She went to the infirmary, but the nurse did not even send her home. To this day, Isabel says she has had problems with her back.

Most women working at the rubber factories did not hold men's jobs, but once the war started, some men's jobs had been broken down into component parts, simplified, or "diluted." Company reports stated that women did the "lighter" work, while men retained the "heavier," better-paying portion of the job. Only later in the war did women completely take over the men's jobs. These women, referred to as "female males" at BFG, were not expected to be permanent replacements for men but were to leave the jobs as soon as men were available. As D. D. Reichow, manager of BFG's industrial relations, explained, "The placing of women on men's jobs is an emergency program to relieve the critical manpower shortage in the Akron area." Under this agreement, the seniority of men and women workers was recorded separately. Thus, even if the women had more "female" seniority, they could not use it to retain the higher-paying men's jobs once men became available.

The women doing men's jobs were to be paid accordingly, but women often had to file grievances to get the higher wages. That situation helped explain the large increase in the number of grievances filed with URW's Local Five (representing workers at BFG) during 1943 and 1944. In 1943, 959 grievances were filed; in 1944, 1,078. In 1942, before large numbers of women were transferred to men's jobs, only 751 grievances had been filed, and in 1945, union records indicated that when most women had been removed from men's jobs, the figure was back to 780. The union was especially eager to pursue these grievances. As one writer for the union newspaper explained, "Industry will try to chisel on paying women the same wages as men for comparable work, in spite of recent War Labor Board decisions laying down that policy."

Sometimes union and company negotiators handled the grievances; if they were unable to reach an agreement, an outside arbitrator was brought in. Most of these cases involved jobs that had been redefined or labor-saving machines or procedures had been introduced into the production process. The situation in B. F. Goodrich's Department 7520 A illustrated the situation. The buffing of fuel cell fittings traditionally had been defined as a man's job because of hazards associated with working on a lathe. When women were assigned to that job, the union insisted that they be paid a man's rate. The company objected, pointing out

An unidentified woman at BFG weaves fire-hose jacketing. The jackets were made in a continuous length and then cut into sections. *B. F. Goodrich Collection.*

that a new method of buffing had been developed, making the job easier. The case was sent to the arbitrator, as was the case of the "screw removal" in which the argument revolved around how men and women did their work. Men used a hand wrench while women used a drill press to remove the screws. The union contended the women should be paid at the same rate as men. The company disagreed, arguing that a machine had made the job easier and, thus, women should be paid at a lower rate. The arbitrator ruled for the union.

Women interested in men's jobs were instructed to apply at the factory personnel department. Special training and other qualifications were considered in addition to seniority when women workers were assigned to male jobs. One union official complained about the favoritism, reporting that at BFG's Mechanical Division foremen were promoting their female "pets" to male jobs. In the end, the union locals agreed to look into the charges on a case-by-case basis.

"Female males" were located throughout Akron's rubber factories. By 1943, three women—Mary Dakon, Amelia Smith, and Mary Rockwood—operated drill presses in Goodyear's machine shop. According to published accounts, the three made the transition effortlessly. "It was due to a shortage of men that women were first given an opportunity to prove their adaptability. Their foreman reports that they are doing a splendid job and have stepped right in without demanding any special adjustments."

The best known of the "female males" were tire builders. Beginning in 1943, a limited number of women were trained for this job. Most made smaller size tires. Mary Amos and Ann Shuman, veterans of sixteen and fifteen years of service respectively, were among the one hundred female tire builders at BFG. Company officials called the performance of these two—and the other ninety-eight female tire builders— "entirely satisfactory." As the *Beacon Journal* reported, "Until a year ago, a tire builder was a big, bruising he-man. Industry, under war pressure, has made the job none too strenuous for a slim girl like Marilyn [Soule of Medina]. She is five feet, six inches tall, weighs 120 pounds. She learned to make small passenger tires in two weeks." A few women made the larger tires. At Firestone, Mary Snader, forty-six, supported an invalid husband and three children by making the larger airplane tires—one of the first women in the rubber industry to do so.

Women taking men's jobs sometimes found hostility in the departments they joined. When women first came to one BFG department, the men refused to work with them. That was not an isolated instance. Union records showed that at BFG in early 1944, about 568 production hours had been lost when men refused to work in protest against putting women on men's jobs. This type of work action became less frequent as more women took over men's jobs.

"Female males" represented only a minority of the women rubber workers, and the union provisions assured that they were *temporary* replacements for the men. When men returned to the department, "female males" were to return to women's jobs, which meant the displaced women took significant wage cuts. When layoffs came, "female males" went first. Male workers were not to be laid off while a woman was working a man's job, according to the union agreements.

Just as the types of jobs filled by women changed over the war, so, too, did the workweek itself. At the beginning of the war, Goodyear,

BFG, Firestone, General, and Seiberling followed what could be termed Depression hours when, as a means of "spreading the work," rubber companies adopted a six-hour day. By 1940, that six-hour day (six days a week) had been written into most United Rubber Worker union contracts. That did not necessarily assure a full thirty-six-hour workweek. In 1940, at BFG, men worked slightly less than thirty-two hours a week, compared with twenty-nine hours for women.

By 1942, severe labor shortages forced a redefinition of the workday. An agreement among labor, management, and government increased the workday to eight hours—without layoffs. By October 1942, the eight-hour day (six days a week) was the rule in the rubber companies. The transition was not without problems. In 1942, when it became apparent that women would be laid off under the new eight-hour day, URW Local Five called for a "readjustment" of hours for women workers in BFG's pontoon and crash pad departments. According to George Bass, URW Local president, women in these departments should be working only six hours a day. "Last week 300 workers in an adjoining department were sent home because there was no work for them to do and we feel that these persons should be given an opportunity to work a normal number of hours per week before other workers are put on an overtime basis." The women in those departments disagreed. A company spokesperson said that 95 percent of the women in the crash pad department had signed a petition asking that they be kept on an eight-hour day.

In spite of that petition, the long hours did represent a hardship for many women workers who had to balance home responsibilities and a

Goodyear made a line of unusual products, such as the decoy vehicles pictured here. Women were involved in this production as well. *Goodyear Collection.*

BFG women workers "walk away" a pneumatic float (pontoon) used by the Engineering Corps for constructing temporary bridges. The women are (clockwise from left front) Jeanne Ater, Relta Bull, Eva Dotson, Kathryn Durbin, Ruth Harold, Frances Insalago, Georgene Jones, Thelma Keith, Madalene Lewis, Lucilla Mears, Marguerite Petros, Goldie Roop, Anna Smallwood, Anna Slupholm, Ruth Sutter and Velma Wood. *B. F. Goodrich Collection.*

forty-eight-hour week in the rubber factories. As many women workers reported to the Women's Bureau, Saturday work was a particular hardship. Saturday was their only day for doing laundry and housekeeping. Thus, at least some of the absenteeism was attributed to those who stayed home to catch up with their household chores.

When the labor shortage was particularly acute and when government contracts demanded overtime, rubber companies could and did use women seven days a week. In 1942, BFG asked to use women seven days a week in the boats, pontoons, crash pads, barrage balloons, hose, belting, and gas mask departments. Sunday work for women was relatively rare during the war, but when it was required, women workers in some departments made Sunday work a treat. In Goodyear's Department 380, Plant Three, the women brought in food to share in a lunchtime "picnic."

The work environment at the rubber factories was defined by both the men and the women. Men controlled the structured channels of authority; women altered their work environment informally, working either through friendship networks to deal with shared problems or individually. Thus, the local War Manpower Commission, the local and national union leadership, and corporate officers, all men, determined the number of hours worked. Corporate officers—in conjunction with union representatives—analyzed and established the job parameters. Wages and piecework rates affecting both male and female jobs were negotiated by men in the union and company. Many of the conditions within the departments were dictated by men as well. The male company engineers, chemists, and physicians determined the acceptable health risks women faced when they determined what chemicals and procedures would be followed in production. Likewise, these same individuals determined what safety equipment would be issued to reduce the risk of accidents or contamination. In most departments, male foremen settled disputes, oversaw production, determined acceptable job performance, and decided which women would qualify for men's jobs. A few women—those who held supervisory or union positions—were allowed into this structured power environment.

This structured system often put women at a disadvantage. The union did little to eliminate the two-tier pay system based on gender and gender-defined work that existed in the rubber factories. Women, because they held women's jobs, were always paid considerably less than men. Before the war, women were paid approximately 60 percent what the men earned. In 1940, for example, women workers in Akron's rubber factories making tires and tubes made 73.8 cents per hour, in an average 30.3-hour week, for about $22.34 per week. In contrast, men made $1.118 per hour in an average 33.5-hour week to earn $37.41. Almost twice as many women could be found in other rubber goods production, which paid far less. In those areas, pay for women ranged from 36.3 cents per hour for toy production ($12.60 a week) to 50.8 cents per hour for mechanical goods production ($17.73 per week), according to Labor Department statistics.

In 1942, tire and tube production continued to be the best-paid jobs in the rubber industry. Women in Akron plants made 89.9 cents per hour but were losing ground, compared to men. Men in Akron tire production made $1.366 per hour. Thus, in 1940, women in Akron in tire and tube production made 66.0 percent of what men did. By 1942, that figure had dropped to 65.8 percent.

The new war products had meant fairly good wages for women, although lower than those earned in the tire/tube department. Women in Akron's balloon departments made an average of 72.8 cents per hour (compared to $1.047 for men). Women making self-sealing tanks made almost as much but far less than the men working in the same department: 85.4 cents per hour, compared to $1.215.

Between 1942 and 1944, a large number of jobs done by women were converted to piecework. The reasoning behind that decision was simple: piecework would increase efficiency and productivity. The most productive workers would receive the greatest amount of money. Workers' attitudes toward to piecework varied. Grace Hanlon saw it as a negative development—"Piece work. They worked women like dogs." Margaret Cooney saw it as a benefit because she should make more money to support her two children. The union handled piecework grievances on a case-by-case basis and was fairly successful in winning adjustments.

Women who did not want to go through the grievance process took more direct action. At General, for example, about 225 women in the life belt department went on strike in May 1943 to protest piecework without some sort of base guarantee. After rejecting a mediator's offer, the women returned to work a few days later with a settlement more to their liking.

In a particularly bitter strike in June 1942, Goodyear women walked off the job after the company announced plans to initiate piecework in the department making flotation bags, assault and escape boats, and life vests. The illegal sit-down strike soon spread as women (and a few men) refused to work until the piecework issue was resolved. The women saw the issue as a matter of survival. The new rates, they argued, would cut their earnings considerably. But to the company, the union, and the community, their strike action was illegal and unpatriotic, and women workers should follow appropriate procedures. Mediators eventually resolved the situation but not before the newspaper chided the 375 striking women. "The girls had their eyes glued on a fat envelope and Uncle Sam could go to hell," the *Beacon* editorialized.

The strikes at General and Goodyear were the most publicized examples of female unity; many work stoppages were not reported. Over three months in 1945, for example, women in various departments at BFG stopped work to protest wage decisions. The three-and-a-half-hour work stoppage on February 23, 1945, was typical. Ten "girls" refused to work in protest of a newly adopted wage rate, according to union records.

Men also determined how women did their jobs, which usually did not cause a problem because female workers had long before made the innovations needed to do the work. The problems arose when women took over new jobs. Sometimes problems developed because a work station was designed for men. John Thomas, chairman of Firestone, observed that certain manufacturing procedures were inappropriate for women, most of whom were smaller than the male workers. Women workers were using air hammers on a bench "and when the air hammer . . . [was] applied, they [women workers] bounced all over the bench." The workstation was too high for women, he explained. Once Thomas recognized the problem, engineers were called in to correct it. "Temporary arrangements were made for them to stand on about 8 inches of ply board, and this relieved the awkward position very much, and the girls were exceedingly pleased to have this help. "How anyone can go through a plant and see a thing of this kind and let it pass is beyond me," Thomas said.

Because male engineers defined the jobs, they also determined the level of health hazards that women workers would face. The manufacture of rubber products had always involved risks associated with the use of potentially hazardous chemicals, solvents, and cements. What made World War II production different was that such a large number of women were exposed to these potentially hazardous chemicals, solvents, and cements and that production often took place in areas that lacked adequate ventilation.

Women who worked in the plants during World War II worked with solvents that contained benzene. Frances Olechnowicz, who became a safety engineer at Goodyear after the war, reported that benzene was used in barrage balloon production, where she worked, and that there was another compound, 866, that was "stronger than benzene. We used to wash our hands in it. We had black cement on our hands and our arms." Agnes Lackney reported using benzene in Firestone's pontoon department as well. As a result, Agnes said, some of the women who worked with her got sick.

A range of physical problems were associated with chemicals, but by far the most common was dermatitis. Shortly after the war, a Firestone executive estimated that dermatitis accounted for almost 90 percent of the occupational disease claims and suggested that the company research "occupational dermatitis" in the hopes of eliminating the problem.

Women were far more likely to have problems with rashes than men, according to a Goodyear doctor. Dermatitis mostly affected the hands. Margaret Cooney ran into the problem in the balloon department and transferred out. At BFG, between January and April 1942, twenty-four women were transferred out of self-sealing tanks because of dermatitis and "malaise headaches."

Women also faced health problems associated with the solvents used in production. URW Local Five kept track of the problems at BFG in early 1942. Twenty-seven union members reported problems; at least seven of these were women. Joan Patterson passed out; Alice Puglisi was sent home sick; Edna Webb reported a kidney condition caused by the solvent fumes. The Goodrich doctor told Julia McFarland, who became ill from the fumes, she could return to work but must avoid solvents. Elizabeth Thorne, who was out sick because of her work with solvents, was advised by a Goodrich doctor to quit her job. She did.

Agnes Lackney remembered the problem in Firestone's pontoon production room. Although she never had symptoms, she remembered that many of her female coworkers got dizzy and broke out in rashes. The workers called it "rubber poisoning," but the Firestone doctors told them there was no such thing.

The companies dealt with health issues in a variety of ways. Sometimes they tested the blood of women workers exposed to certain chemicals. Frances Golliday never knew why the tests were given and the doctors at Goodyear never volunteered any information—and the women did not ask. She said the women did not understand about the possible health risks; "we [were] so happy to have a job and they [management] were so good to us."

Companies issued protective clothing, but, according to testimony given at a conference dealing with health hazards in the rubber industry, "the average woman worker is less efficiently protected by clothing than

Three unidentified women work on the ten-man rubber landing boats at Firestone. The boats, which saved many men during the war, could be inflated in seconds. *Cleveland Press Collection.*

the average man." Part of the problem was that the protective garb did not fit the women properly. It was typically one-size-fits-all and both genders, which meant that it was difficult for women to work in the company-issued clothing. In addition, some women did not like to wear the protective clothing.

Sometimes they simply did not want to wear the uncomfortable clothing. Economic factors also entered into their reasoning. Most safety gear was issued free to employees who faced hazards on the job, but not always. At Goodyear Aircraft in 1943, for example, the safety division began to urge women to wear a "headdress" at their work, but the women workers had to buy the equipment. Bob Fickes, safety director for Plants A and B, told women workers that they should purchase the headdress that was "on sale at the employees' stores." In still other instances, vanity entered into the picture, or so claimed Goodyear's women's personnel adviser Dorothy F. Markle. She explained that women will "wear safety shoes and safety glasses, but they all put a noble battle for at least one little curl to protrude from under safety hats because 'I like it that way.'"

The companies often reminded the women workers that in spite of the ill-fitting nature of the safety gear, the financial hardship it sometimes posed, and the personal factors that might work against it, they should always wear safety equipment. In fact, many of the stories directed at women took all these factors into account. One short feature in the *Wingfoot Clan* addressed the issues specifically affecting women:

FOOT PROTECTION: Safety shoes should be worn. A new light-weight attractive style, especially for women, is now available.

EYE PROTECTION: Adequate eye protection should be worn. Lightweight safety goggles and rimless good-looking safety spectacles are now on the market.

OUTER GARMENTS: Women should wear outer garments designed to minimize the possibility of entanglements in machinery. There should be no loose sleeves, full skirts or blouses, ties, lapels or cuffs on garments.

HEAD PROTECTION: The hair should be completely enclosed in an approved cap, hairnet or bandana.

HAND PROTECTION: Hand coverings of a suitable material and design should be worn to prevent cuts, burns, and skin poisoning. Gloves, however, should not be worn while working around moving machinery.

JEWELRY: No jewelry of any kind should be worn around machinery or electrical equipment.

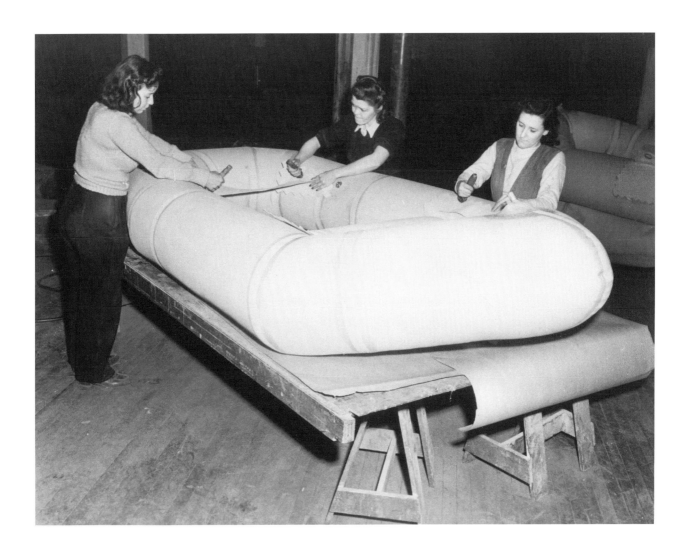

On most jobs, women were not required to wear uniforms—provided their clothing did not pose a safety risk. How that was defined depended a good deal on the department. Many women rubber workers wore slacks. "Thelma McClung" humorously explained the reasoning behind this: "I have to wear pants because they tell us dresses are hazardous to women workers. Of course, the trouble with wearing pants is that a girl can't show her individuality. How is anybody going to know that a girl is a glamour girl if she's garbed in mechanized attire? Yes, I'm strong for slacks for girls working on war materials. We can't crawl over the floor and on piles of stock conveniently if we wear . . . dresses or other 'accountrements.' If we do, we're liable to break a leg."

When Margaret Cooney was in the balloon room, she wore jeans—something that took some getting used to. "I never thought I'd get used to wearing them but after we wore them for a while—it's just like everything else, you get used to it." When she transferred to gas masks, there

Ida Smith (left), Deborah Parvin (middle), and Elizabeth Stumfoll work assembling life rafts at BFG. *B. F. Goodrich Collection.*

were no restrictions on clothing. "Sometimes I wore pants, sometimes I didn't," she remembered. Isabel Moran wore only trousers when she worked at Firestone.

Tressie McGee preferred to wear a uniform and bought two from Goodyear's employee stores. The uniforms came in two varieties: "natty, navy blue stock suits and farmerette coveralls." By 1943, Goodyear Aircraft required women to wear uniforms. The one-piece suit, available at the employee store, cost $4.35, and a matching hat sold for $1.25.

Thelma Bolen never wore a uniform. She always wore trousers, usually topped off with a sweater. Wearing a sweater to work, however, was not necessarily the patriotic thing to do. The Office of War Information called sweaters an enemy of output: "It isn't just a rumor that a tightly sweatered working companion takes a man's eyes off his machine." Thelma wasn't concerned about sex appeal. She was just trying to keep warm in the drafty Goodyear Aircraft plant that "didn't have a lot of heat."

Women had more trouble in the summer in the rubber factories than in the winter. The rubber plants were hot—very hot. "Winters I don't mind," Betty Pinter said, "but the summers were intolerable. For me, I pass out in extreme heat. I always did, even as a child. I can't stand heat." The salt tablets didn't help much, and rubber itself made the situation worse. Betty remembered that "rubber keeps the heat and you were surrounded by it."

In 1943, Goodyear Aircraft was literally flooded. Here women and men workers are standing in the water, waiting to get into work. *Goodyear Collection.*

Individual departmental supervisors did not have much control over the temperature, but they did have control over many aspects of the women's workday. In Akron's rubber factories in World War II, supervisors were important authority figures. The largest number of those supervisors were men—white men. Whether the women represented a minority of the workers in the department or the greatest number of the operatives, the supervisors were most likely to be male. Women supervisors were in departments traditionally associated with a female labor force.

The rubber companies blamed the women workers themselves for the lack of female supervisors. According to the company, women workers did not want female supervisors—and neither did the male workers. In negotiations held in 1943 the union and the company agreed on that point:

> [D. D.] Reichow [BFG manager of industrial relations]: We don't feel we want to go into women supervision yet. I don't know that you want us to really.
> [George] Bass [president of URW Local 5]: I don't believe in a woman supervisor over women or men.

That attitude continued throughout much of the war. A notable exception was Goodyear's Silver Squadron, a select group of women who were trained for supervision. They were to be the female version of the Squadron, an elite group of men who were trained for supervisory jobs.

Foremen influenced women's pay by approving downtime, time when piecework was not available, and selecting the women who would be placed on men's jobs. They mediated wage disputes before the grievance stage. Usually these disputes were handled informally. Agnes Lackney at Firestone had to argue with her foreman to get all the money she deserved. "I remember arguing with my boss to get my money.... When we made out our cards and turned it into pieces and if we had time that we lost and we didn't have pieces to go through there, we had downtime. We only got day work for it. We averaged out our day work and our piecework and added up for our day's pay and he wouldn't give us our day work. So I had to argue with him to get it." The foreman did not have the final say. If the women workers did not feel that the dollar amount was correct, they could file a grievance with the union.

Foremen also decided which women qualified for the better-paying men's jobs. Seniority was not the primary consideration. Only the best qual-ified women—those physically capable of the work or with special skills—were to be given those jobs. These vague job specifications allowed

During World War II, women were allowed to be a part of Goodyear's prestigious Squadron, individuals trained for supervision. To differentiate it from the male group, Goodyear dubbed its female organization, the "Silver Squadron." The squadrons operated in both the tire factory and the aircraft facility. Pictured is the first graduating class of Goodyear Aircraft's Squadron (1944). *Collection of Sandra Mondrich.*

the foremen room to show favoritism—or that is what the URW argued. The URW received complaints about foremen promoting their "pets" but found such charges difficult to pursue.

The complaints of favoritism and the problems associated with pay concerns illustrated that the foremen's job required judgment and interpersonal communication skills. Some foremen were ill equipped to meet the challenges of the job. Few were trained in conflict management or knew how to deal with the harassment suffered by so many women in the rubber factories. Few were sensitive to racial problems, and fewer still knew how to defuse potentially explosive situations.

Foremen discovered that conflict among women could arise for far different reasons than among men and that solving such problems took a good deal of patience. A personnel officer at one rubber company explained how to handle such situations: "There are many problems who come to us, claiming someone is trying to beat them out of the job, or has been telling tales about them, or is just plain ornery. It takes diplomacy to handle these women. Usually just crying on someone's shoulder solves the case."

Harassment was common in the rubber factories during World War II. Older male workers played tricks or teased the young, inexperienced women workers. Betty Pinter came to Goodrich young and naive, the perfect target for jokes, teasing, and harassment. She remembered one time in particular: "They [the men workers] sent me to the tool room to pick up some tools my boss wanted me to get. And, of course, everybody was in on the joke. Poor, dumb Betty. I went to get a sky hook, and a left-handed monkey wrench, and a fallopian tube. And I asked for them. I come back with a ha-ha-ha from everybody in the area and the tool room man. How dumb can you be at twenty-one?"

Frances Golliday remembered the jokes the men told. "I was just a young kid. They were older men and, of course, they teased me and told me all kinds of stories and jokes and dirty jokes and stuff like that. Tried to embarrass me is what they tried to do." Frances and Betty never told their foremen about these jokes. They just dealt with the harassment, typically by ignoring the comments or wising up to the pranks.

Some women found it difficult to forge a good relationship with the foremen. Verna Haag found she needed to argue with her boss at Firestone, "but that's only natural," she explained. Sally Foore and her co-workers even acted up to get back at their supervisor, Red Spiker. "He was a peeker and a watcher of us workers. We did not like that at all. Sometimes we would be lazy on purpose to irritate him."

Finding the right relationship with the supervisor included finding the right vocabulary. In one exchange at BFG between a foreman and a woman worker, the woman made a "smutty remark" and her foreman slapped her. The union demanded that the supervisor be removed. The foreman was placed on another job but not demoted, indicating that the company believed the worker was at fault. As BFG's D. D. Reichow argued, "This whole thing—so-called alleged slugging or slapping—was the result of some remark the girl made. What kind of people are we dealing with anyway?"

The slapping incident was further complicated when the foreman urged some of the women workers to take his side and pressure the woman to drop her grievance. Here race entered the picture. The union charged that the foreman, who "must have a following among the Negro girls," asked at least one African American woman to approach the

At Goodyear, African American women were integrated into production departments with only limited difficulty. This picture shows two unidentified women, one Caucasian and the other African American, working together. *Goodyear Collection.*

worker who filed the grievance and urge her to withdraw it. The African American woman even wrote the statement of withdrawal.

Incidents involving slapping were rare. Incidents pitting one race against another were more common. Again, the foremen had to defuse potentially explosive situations, and many of them were ill-equipped to handle the situation. The introduction of a single African American woman into production was not usually accompanied by hostility. Inez Rogers reported that her transition into the BFG workplace was effortless. She quickly made friends with the white women she worked with and liked the work environment in the gas mask department. Goodrich soon brought African American women into other departments. By 1942,

African Amercan women were working "in at least half a dozen departments where they had said before they could not be placed."

Initially Firestone segregated African American women in certain production jobs. In 1943, seven African American women were employed at Firestone, all in the third-shift paint spray booth. By mid-1943, Firestone was preparing to hire and train more African American women but was not sure how to proceed. J. W. Dean Jr., Firestone's production manager, suggested dropping the policy of segregation. "My recommendation is that we disregard this attempt at segregation and place them [African American women] in the school . . . , getting them eventually into the assembly operations." Apparently Dean's suggestion was followed.

In spite of this planning, integration of departments did not always go smoothly. At Goodyear Tire and Rubber, for example, union members walked out rather than work with an African American. The strike was short-lived, and when the workers returned, blacks and whites in that department worked together without further incident.

Most problems arose when African Americans first joined a department. At BFG, for example, sixteen African American women transferred into Department 7520 to work on buffing but found a hostile environ-

During World War II, African American women joined the production work force. Before the war, they had been relegated to janitorial and maintenance jobs. *Goodyear Collection.*

ment and refused to work. The union insisted it was not a work stoppage. The African American women simply did not know how to handle the situation and apparently neither the union nor the foreman intervened to defuse the tension. The African American women continued to work in the department and apparently faced no other problems.

Sometimes, the company itself exacerbated the situation. George Bass, president of URW Local Five, reported that a foreman at BFG warned that if the white workers refused work eight hours, the company would bring in African Americans who would. Bass said he told the foreman, "Bring them in. We'll work with them."

The amount of supervision and latitude given women depended on a supervisor's personality. Some did not supervise closely and productivity was adversely affected, as was the case at Firestone's Aircraft Wings Building. One company official observed, "I saw only two supervisors in the whole place. There was one instance of horseplay by five girls working on one wing, with no supervisor in sight . . . Several groups were engaged in conversation, and one young boy at the crib nearest the northeast corner of he building was jerking the chair by inches from under a girl seated at the table by the crib door trying to work."

Gladys Burton was one of the African American women recruited by Goodyear Aircraft in 1941. She recalled that the training period was especially long because management was unsure how the integration of the workforce should take place. By July 1941 she was on the job making airplane wings at the aircraft hangar but remembered that working at Goodyear Aircraft left a lot to be desired. The working conditions were harsh as was some of the racism she faced at the plant. She left Goodyear in 1942 and went to work at BFG, where she had heard conditions for African Americans were better. She worked at BFG for the next ten years. *Collection of Gladys Gibson.*

When women workers were unhappy with foremen's actions or behavior, they could turn to their union, but the union did not always pursue their complaints. If the complaint affected only women, as was the case in charges of favoritism, the union was not likely to pursue the matter vigorously. As one union officer admitted, he "kissed them off." In contrast, women's complaints about not being paid equal wages for male jobs were likely to be vigorously pursued because the issue would affect male workers when they returned from the war.

The uneven response illustrated that the union was controlled by men and not always sympathetic to women's concerns, even though women had long been members of the union and would continue to be members after the war. And it happened even though the union adopted resolutions specifically designed to prevent such problems: "The United Rubber Workers of America in convention assembled reaffirm their uncompromising stand against all discrimination whether it be race, creed, color or sex."

Women were especially important in inspection. Pictured is part of Firestone's final inspection table, where metallic belt links are inspected and boxed for shipment in 1942. The women on the right are testing each link; each worker tested thousands of links on each shift. The women on the left did the packaging. The man to the right is the supervisor. *Cleveland Press Collection.*

Women had little voice in their local or international union. Few women held union positions, and even those who did hold a position did not necessarily enjoy job security. For example, Lola Broughton, a popular BFG committeewoman representing women workers, was slated to be replaced by a man. After a petition signed by thirty-three workers protested the move, Local Five "clarified" the decision, keeping Lola on the job and adding a committeeman, James Saunders, to represent an unspecified "certain group of workers."

Broughton's situation was handled quietly, without a work stoppage. Women workers, however, were ready to walk off the job to support a committeewoman. In 1944, three hundred Goodyear Aircraft workers walked off the job in sympathy for their committeewoman, Dora Kenner, who had been dismissed. The women went back the next day, but the company and the union met to discuss Dora's grievances.

The Goodyear Aircraft walkout and the BFG petition reflected the tension some women workers felt toward the union. The URW dismissed this as "inexperience" on the part of certain women, who had to be taught to "conduct themselves as militant union people." But the problem was not that simple. Certain women workers became increasingly dissatisfied with how the union handled their concerns, issues, and problems. That frustration erupted in a brief unsanctioned strike of women workers at Firestone. As one striker explained, "This is a protest strike as far as we are concerned, but it's a protest against [union] leaders drawing fat pay who have failed to fight our cause."

A female culture developed and operated outside the official male-controlled lines in the industrial patriarchy. Women created this culture through their informal networks of friends, relatives, and acquaintances at work. These women redefined their jobs and created work conditions more conducive to female communication and work styles. Female networks shared one end: to improve the work environment for women workers. Sometimes they accomplished this goal through methods such as the "suggestion" programs at the various rubber companies. The number of women participating never equaled the number of men, but the companies agreed that the quality of the suggestions submitted by women was consistently better. Goodrich used 40 percent of the suggestions submitted by women but only 34 percent of all suggestions submitted by men. Women's suggestions typically dealt with production associated with female workers. Mary Brown, who earned the title "prize suggestion girl" at Goodyear, suggested a change in the manufacture of tool repair kits for life rafts that saved one thousand woman-hours annually. Marjorie Hess earned $20 when she developed a special wrench for tightening valves on life rafts, thereby reducing the time needed for that operation. Opal Davis, also of Goodyear, won $20 for her suggestion that improved a mold in the fuel tank department. At Goodyear Aircraft, Grace Pence came up with an idea that helped with the production of the Corsairs. At Goodyear Tire and Rubber, Rettie Worstell improved gas mask productivity considerably when she suggested adding a "hemmer" attachment to the sewing machines in that department. She earned $140 for that idea. Rosemary Olenick and Alice Colletta used hair-curler technology to help improve production in Goodyear Aircraft's Department 345. They had found it difficult to keep fabric taut and reasoned that the heat from an industrial-strength hair curler might do the trick. It did, and the suggestion improved production throughout Goodyear Aircraft and Great Britain's aircraft industry as well. Grace Carrington, an African American, submitted several suggestions and "collected cash for her efforts," the company newspaper reported.

In most instances, however, women workers operated outside the formal factory structure to improve work conditions. Each department was an environment unto itself. Where large numbers of women worked together, friendship networks developed. These networks could enhance the working conditions but also could act as barriers to new women who entered the department. A *Beacon Journal* reporter explained, "The women form cliques in their department and the new women coming on the job must successfully pass a test period before being accepted as one of the girls."

Each department had its own female culture. Some departments included older, more experienced women workers. Younger women tended to avoid those departments. Margaret Cooney explained, "A lot of the older women worked in different departments because they could probably make more in boxing tires and things. We was always afraid to sign up for any of those jobs." It was a matter of the work environment, not the jobs themselves. Margaret continued, "Because they were older women and they had a clique [she and her friends tended to avoid those departments]. Every place you go, most places have cliques and if you're not in with them, then, why, you feel out of place."

Younger female workers gravitated to certain departments. Margaret Cooney said that in fuel cells most of the women were young, and they "kind of stuck together." She counted ten to fifteen women in her immediate friendship network at work. Although the work was strenuous, having the female support network in the department made the workday go faster.

Verna Haag found friends among the women who had children. Verna had two youngsters when she went to work at Firestone. Quite a few

BFG made thousands of life rafts during World War II. Women were responsible for much of this production, and many women submitted suggestions that made production of life rafts easier and more efficient. *B. F. Goodrich Collection.*

of the women in her department had children, "and we all seemed to have the same thoughts and things." Like Margaret, Verna wanted to avoid the "hassles" of working in departments where older women predominated.

The female networks could also create a hostile environment, as Thelma Bolen found at Goodyear Aircraft. A woman who was not in her department targeted Thelma for harassment. She started spreading rumors about her, accusing her of wearing "falsies," and the eighteen-year-old found herself the object of unwanted attention. "I . . . [didn't] want people—men—coming up here looking at me and approaching me," Thelma explained. She told her male supervisor about the harassment but he did nothing. Finally, Thelma decided to handle the situation herself. She confronted the woman. Words led to pushing; pushing ended in fighting. As Thelma remembered, "Well, she hauled off and hit me and, when she did that, I was all over her. 'Course we were on the floor and fighting and everything." Both were called upstairs to explain. Thelma was given a warning, but the other woman was suspended for two weeks. The other woman never returned to Goodyear Aircraft, and Thelma was able to work in peace.

Margaret Cooney remembered one woman who got angry at a fellow worker, and "she threw a bucket of hot nylon on her. She almost got fired for that." Margaret said this particular woman was an example of some of the "pretty hot tempered people that would work in the shops." Marie Stephens was another "hot-tempered" woman. The executive board of URW Local Five held her responsible for much of the dissension in her department at BFG. Nonetheless, George Bass, president of the local, urged Leah Kapusinski, Mildred Benson, and Anna Rutkes to cooperate with Marie for the "betterment of our organization": "Although we believe that you girls have been trying to get along with Marie, we feel that perhaps we might go a little further in recognizing that Marie has an unusual temper and perhaps she should be treated a little differently from many others in the department."

Only the most extreme hostility was brought to the attention of the union and the foremen. The more typical problem women workers faced was not being able to fit in. Margaret Cooney remembered never really "fitting in" to the balloon room or gas masks. "I really never got close to, I had a couple of good friends but not in the gas masks. I was really young and naive at that time and some of those women were older and they talked a lot different than what I did."

When women could not adjust to the work environment within a department, they could transfer out. If that wasn't possible, the women could keep to themselves or find one or two friends who supported them at work. Betty Pinter, who worked at Goodrich, found it difficult to deal with the language in her department. "I didn't grow up with people swearing. It was not something done in our home. It was not something done in the children's home. And there was quite a lot of it.... They were kind of a rough bunch of people," Betty explained. She dealt with the situation by finding and keeping to a small circle of friends. When V-E Day came, she left Goodrich—and the people who worked there—behind forever.

Many women did not so easily give up their wartime friendships, which still invoke warm, positive feelings. Thelma Bolen remembered two friends from Goodyear, Mack and Mary, who helped her acclimate to the industrial environment. "They used to call us 'triple double trouble.' Not because we got into any trouble but because we wouldn't let anyone cause us any problems." Margaret Cooney O'Leary still calls Dorothy Rightmyer her friend. Although Dorothy was ten years older and the two had different personalities, they became best friends. They often worked together during the war and for many years after. Dorothy "was kind of a coarse-talking woman and I was always very meek and very shy. I was shy, really shy when I went to work. And she used to cuss and swear a lot and I used to say, 'Dorothy, that isn't nice. Why do you do that?' So she always said I was so good for her because I was always so shy because if anybody said anything too mean to me I wouldn't ever pay any attention to them. She would always stick up for me all the time. She said you let everybody take advantage of you. If I did, I didn't know it."

Isabel Moran and Jean Haig were inseparable at Firestone's Aviation Products Division. The two met at training school and worked together throughout the war. Similarly, Billie Schott at Goodyear Aircraft and her cousin quickly found five friends at training school. The seven worked and played together, and six of them lived together.

The female friendship networks illustrated the positive ways women dealt with the industrial patriarchy. But women also found other, less positive ways to deal with the conditions around them—ways that the union, company, and community found unacceptable.

By far the most common such method was absenteeism. In the rubber factories of Akron during World War II, the rate of female absenteeism was almost twice as high as that of men. In 1943, the absentee rate for Akron was the highest in the state—8.9 percent. Typically, the absenteeism rate for women hovered around 6.5 percent (compared to 2.5 percent in peacetime), although certain companies veered considerably from this figure. For example, Goodyear reported that women's absenteeism reached 11.5 percent in May 1943.

The War Manpower Commission cited several reasons for women's high absentee rate: illness (the worker's or a family member's); housework and personal duties; problems with transportation; "lack of carefully planned production and good supervision"; failure to take the war seriously; excessive drinking; and "general effects of wartime prosperity."

The companies found several ways to deal with female absenteeism. BFG established a committee that was to devise a plan to reduce absenteeism among women. Not one woman was appointed to that committee. Some companies issued posters to remind men and women of "their sacred responsibilities on the production line." One company carried

(*Opposite*) General Tire and Rubber's labor-management committee hung this display to encourage workers to meet production goals. At the end of the week, if the quota was met, a mortar sent up a bomb that notified Akron—loudly—that another General shift had done its job producing tires for army planes, combat cars, and other military units. *Cleveland Press Collection.*

on "presenteeism" campaigns to reward workers. Together with the union, it sponsored rallies. In one of the first rallies honoring BFG workers, two African American women were honored: Lola Smith and Gwendolyn Steward. Neither had missed a day since starting work in 1942.

Part of the reasoning behind these campaigns was to improve the attitude of the women workers toward the company. A worker who identified with the company was less likely to be absent or leave its employ. As a reporter for the city's newspaper saw it, "It all winds up with the worker getting pretty fond of her company because they do so much for her—and because they remember their production success depends on whether all the women and all the men in their company are happy."

Despite the corporate efforts, absenteeism remained high throughout the war. But absenteeism was only one symptom of the deep, unresolved problems among women workers. The most extreme way indi-

On June 28, 1942, Goodyear hosted a "Rub Out the Axis" rally. In this photo, the crowd is gathered around a lifeboat that saved three navy flyers in 1942. The three floated on the South Seas for thirty-four days on a boat that had been produced by Goodyear—primarily by women. *Goodyear Collection.*

An unidentified Goodyear worker demonstrates how the life vest operates to an Army flier. Women production workers were often used in publicity photos like this one; they also had opportunities to see and meet celebrities and war heroes touring Akron rubber factories. *Goodyear Collection.*

vidual women workers had to deal with problems at work or with balancing home with the long factory hours was simply to leave. Turnover among women rubber workers was high. Local War Manpower Commissioner Harry Markle estimated the rate as high as 50 percent in December 1942, that was probably an overestimate. Rubber company reports were more conservative. They placed the turnover rate for women in 1944 at 7.8 percent. Individual companies and divisions had more of a problem. In 1944, Firestone's Aviation Products Division had a female turnover rate of 9.5 percent. That represented a substantial number because more than 50 percent of this division's workforce was women.

Typically, those who left, left quickly. Firestone found that more than 90 percent of the women who left its Aviation Products Division had worked less than a year. One published account argued that the greatest portion of the women who left were married, but corporate reports did not substantiate that conclusion. Firestone used exit interviews to determine why workers left the company. The most common reason given was "leaving town," a reflection of the high turnover rate among those recruited from outside the area. An unspecified "dissatisfaction" explained another large group who left. Almost as large were the number who left because of "home duties." "Poor health" explained why another substantial group left the company.

Women who left often did so with misgivings. Tressie McGee had to leave Goodyear for reasons that might be classified as poor health; her doctor told her that her injured leg would never heal if she continued to work. Inez Rogers didn't want to leave but she could not tolerate the heat at Goodrich's Miller plant. Pregnant Thelma Bolen left after she passed out on the job. She did not want a job change and took a medical leave instead. Billie Schott left to get married.

Notwithstanding the absenteeism and the turnover, the largest number of the women who worked in the rubber factories during World War II seemed to truly enjoy their jobs. Some liked the work because they were allowed to do things that they had never tried before. Lucy Capozzi worked on B-29 bombers and Corsairs. She explained, "I loved my work and found it to be very interesting after attending Goodyear traine [*sic*] school."

Others enjoyed contributing to the war effort. Frances Spain, who worked in a dress shop before coming to Goodyear Aircraft, thought her work keeping track of the steel and aluminum tubing for blimps and planes in Plant B's materials control department was important and exciting. "It's far more exciting to think that the material you handle is going to our fighting men rather than dress goods going to the seamstress for some dresses. I like my job at Aircraft and if it ever becomes necessary for me to return to a store counter, I'm afraid I'll find it rather monotonous for a while." Sally Foore agreed. In Goodyear's balloon room, she felt "a sense of accomplishment. It was tedious work, but we acquired knowledge to build something out of almost nothing (some thin rubber and cement)."

More, however, emphasized the camaraderie fostered by war work. Clarice Douglas had come from Spencer, West Virginia, to work at Goodyear Aircraft in 1942. Her fondest memory of working there was the people: "Bonding of Relationships with many people[,] those of my age, older ones who took over as parents and provided much wisdom, encouragement, protection. Each left me with some memory to help form who I am today."

In addition, the sense of patriotism was empowering. The media, the rubber companies, and the community all told the women that they were doing something important for the war effort. Josephine Heacox had worked in a drugstore but went to Goodyear Aircraft during the war. "My job in the drugstore seemed so useless compared to what I might be doing in a war plant," she told a reporter for the company's newspaper. Isabel Bitner emphasized that patriotism was a key element but not the only one. Her fondest memory of working at Firestone was "having a job, making more money than I had ever made, and feeling that I was contributing to the war effort." Ernestine Rogers echoed those sentiments when describing her time at Goodyear Aircraft and Goodrich's Miller plant: "I'm sure I felt proud to be working on war-related material. I remember most of the workers being pleasant and I was away from home, on my own for the first time."

The factory was a dual environment, the structure defined by men, the informal network of friends and relatives defined by women. Through informal networks of friends and family, women workers were able to exercise their autonomy and develop a culture of their own. Friendship and family networks helped to foster a conducive work environment.

Female networks, however, were not always enough. The high rates of absenteeism and turnover illustrated that not all women were happy in the factory work environment or were able to balance the demands of

On December 7, 1942, Goodyear employees remembered the first anniversary of the bombing of Pearl Harbor by the Japanese. Nearly two-hundred clergymen from various denominations participated in a series of services. Pictured is William H. Huber, pastor of the First Presbyterian Church, praying with the employees of the balloon department. *Goodyear Collection.*

their home responsibilities with a forty-eight-hour workweek. The growing number of grievances filed by women showed a tension and dissatisfaction that individual workers were facing in their departments. The women-led strikes illustrated how women working together were able to deal with shared problems.

When women went into the rubber factories in World War II, they did not surrender any of their other duties and responsibilities. Factory life represented only part of Rosie's existence. She was also a wife and mother with all the duties associated with those roles. Or she was a single woman with far more opportunities for adventure and play. While the single and married women might hold similar jobs at work, they faced quite different lives outside the factory gates.

five

Rosie Outside the Factory Gates

Dolly Bell was just eighteen when she came to Akron from Grants-ville, West Virginia, in 1944. It was a homecoming of a sort. Dolly's mother had moved to Akron to work at Goodyear in 1943, and the teenager spent that first summer with her mother. Too young to apply at any of the rubber factories, Dolly worked at Scot's, a five-and-dime store in downtown Akron. In the fall, she returned home to finish high school. After graduation, she came back to Akron to work. Dolly was hired at Goodrich in 1944, making self-sealing airplane gasoline tanks on the second shift. She quickly made new friends at the plant; her two closest were Greta Sligert and Theresa Bowden. The three soon became known as the "three songbirds" because they loved to sing harmony on the way to lunch. Dolly recalled, "We'd go to lunch singing and I remember one of our favorite songs we would sing—'Put your arms around me, Honey, hold me tight.' I'd sing alto, another would sing soprano, and another would sing tenor."

These young women soon were out enjoying the sights and sounds of the big city of Akron. On weekends, they took in the late-night movies at the Strand, a downtown theater. Dolly remembered, "We'd walk down Main Street to go to the movies and . . . we'd take our buses home. And, of course, we didn't have the fear of walking on the streets or riding on the buses or anything at night back then. There was no problem. We could walk anyplace in Akron." They also enjoyed dances. Dolly seemed to have lots of free time, in spite of working eight hours a day, six days a week. Household demands at her apartment were minimal and the money she made was enough to pay for her adventures with Greta and Theresa.

The story was less bright for Dolly's mother, Almeda, a widow. She had heard about the Akron rubber jobs from relatives who already worked for Goodyear and Firestone. When she came to Akron to work, Almeda left her five children in West Virginia. Like so many other mothers who worked in the rubber companies, Almeda relied on relatives to care for her children while she worked. Her eldest daughter, aged twenty, was already on her own; the other four, aged seventeen, fourteen, eleven, and eight, stayed with their grandmother. Almeda seldom saw the children. She explained, "Well, I didn't get back very much because it was expensive and it was a little rough to get into the area where we lived. We lived back in the country." But Almeda was assured that the children were getting the best possible care: "They were taken care of just fine as if I had been there hovering all the time." Almeda took an apartment when she moved to Akron, but it was a difficult transition—"I didn't drive or anything," she remembered, "and Akron was new to me [so] . . . I stayed in my apartment." She couldn't afford to go out on the town even if she wanted to. Almeda had to send money back home to support her children. The radio provided her greatest entertainment. Of course, she made friends at work, but she seldom saw the women outside the factory. Almeda's relatives from West Virginia became her circle of friends outside of work. They even introduced her to her future husband, who worked at the Taystee Bread Company.

One family. Two different experiences. Dolly found wartime Akron a liberating experience; Almeda, her mother, discovered a less friendly environment. Much of the difference could be ascribed to the age and marital status of the women.

The experiences of Almeda and Dolly were fairly typical for women rubber workers in the city. Married women usually had to maintain their responsibilities at home in addition to their factory jobs. Cooking, cleaning, shopping, and child care left little time to explore the attractions of Akron.

Child care was one of the biggest problems that working mothers had to face. The government, the rubber companies, and the unions had realized early that child care—or the lack of it—was going to be the biggest obstacle to women joining the industrial labor force in this metropolitan area. In the first year of the war, the chief of the War Manpower Commission in Akron had discouraged mothers of young children from applying for the defense industry jobs because of problems associated with child care. Mothers with children under the age of fifteen were specifically asked not to apply for wartime jobs unless they could properly care for their children. That attitude softened as the war continued and the need for women workers increased. The community helped provide child care facilities for at least some of the working mothers.

The largest number of working mothers, however, looked to their families to provide child care. Some mothers from out of town did what Almeda had done; they left the children back home with relatives. Thus, Terry Joe Taylor, two, daughter of Pauline Strader Taylor of Goodyear's Department 304 (quality control, Plant Three), stayed with her grandparents in Weston, West Virginia, while her mother and two aunts moved to Akron to work. Five-year-old Carol Jean Jones, daughter of Margarite Jones of Department 373 (K-ship fins) at Goodyear, had a good time back in Kentucky with her grandmother. "I'm so glad Carol Jean is well taken care of, so I can continue my work without having the slightest worry regarding her welfare," Margarite told the reporter for the company's newspaper.

Far more mothers found family members, usually the maternal grandmother, to watch their children while they worked. Such was the case with Stella Mears, who got a job as a band builder at Goodyear in 1942. Her husband, Richard, worked at a latex products company. But her two children—aged two and four and a half—stayed with her mother, Mrs. S. C. Skiles. Stella explained that without her mother's help, she would not be able to work. "I think mother deserves a lot of credit for keeping the children while we both work. If it weren't for her help it would be impossible for me to do my part in a war industry, as it is a problem these days to get household help." The same situation existed for Charlotte Keirns of Department 373 at Goodyear. Her mother watched her grandson Harry, age six. Verna Haag, a young mother of two, lived with her parents when she got her job at Firestone. She worked third shift so she relied on her mother to watch her children, aged eight and nine, while she worked and tried to sleep during the day.

Although the mothers of the female rubber workers appeared to be the most common choice to mind the children, other women looked to other family members to assume that responsibility. For example, before Margaret Cooney used a child care center, she relied on her grandfather to watch her children, aged two and three months. Margaret's grandfather also worked at Goodyear, but on a different shift so the two could share child care responsibilities. They two lived together with the children. Mary Lucille Young had a live-in housekeeper and baby-sitter in her sister Elizabeth Harper, fourteen. Mary, Elizabeth, and Mary's two children moved into a converted gas station. Mary worked first shift, leaving "before dawn every day," while her sister kept house and watched the children.

The rubber companies offered a measure of flexibility in organizing shifts for parents. Mary and Steve Dobso, for example, arranged their work schedules so one parent was at home at all times with their two children, aged six and four. Steve worked at Goodyear Aircraft in final inspection from 11 P.M. to 6:30 A.M. Mary worked from 2 P.M. to 10 P.M. at Goodyear Plant Two. Given the complexity of their lives, working and sleeping had to be carefully scheduled. Steve slept until Mary left for work. Mary slept after returning from work. A similar situation existed for the James E. Johnsons. Mrs. Johnson worked second shift (on rubber boats) and her husband worked third shift (in the balloon room). The arrangement seemed to provide the supervision that their eight children needed. Timing in such situations was not always perfect. Rusha McDaniel, who worked second shift at Goodyear Tire and Rubber, and her husband, who was on first shift at Imperial Electric, tried to arrange things so at least one parent was around for their two sets of twins, Paul and Pauline, eleven, and Carol and Carolyn, three and a half; but that wasn't always possible. She told the reporter for the company newspaper that when neither parent was around, a neighbor would watch the children.

Child care problems cut across racial lines, but patterns tended to be similar. Inez Rogers, for example, turned to a relative who also rented a room from her. Ben Harris, a distant relative who worked at General, and his wife lived with Inez and her three children. Mrs. Harris, who did not work outside the home, picked Inez's children up at school and took care of them until Inez returned from work.

When the children were older, mothers often allowed them to stay on their own or to look after the younger children. That apparently worked well for Marian Darrah, who worked making gas masks at Goodyear. Her four children—Donald, ten, Edward, nine, Gerald, eight, and Marjorie, seven—were quite self-sufficient, Marian told the reporter for the company newspaper. "Since their mother was working, the children 'rolled out' of bed each morning and got themselves ready for school."

Some working mothers were forced to look outside the family unit for individuals to watch their children. Some advertised for baby-sitters in the classifieds of the city's newspaper or the company's periodical. Women who were willing to watch children also placed advertisements. For example, Mrs. Arthur Partenheimer advertised her willingness to watch several children of Goodyear workers. Other offers in the company periodicals were made by unidentified individuals. One offered to care for a daughter of a mother working second shift; another offered room and board to a woman working first shift in exchange for light housekeeping and child care in the evening, presumably during the second shift.

Although relatives and neighbors helped working mothers with their children, instances of child neglect and juvenile delinquency became more numerous. The city's Family Service Society and Office of Civilian Defense found parents who "drag home from the factories at night, too weary to perform the customary household duties, too worn out to pay much heed to their youngsters' up-bringing. And these are youngsters who can no longer be sent over to auntie's for the day while mother works—because auntie has a job, too." As early as 1942, humane officers and county and city law officials were reporting an increase in the number of child-neglect cases. While investigating such claims, humane officers found "unspeakably dirty" conditions in homes that had been livable before. The difference, according to the officer, was that the mother was doing war work and not keeping up with her home responsibilities. Some women were also unable to exert discipline in their homes. As a result, "children are running the streets wild, more than ever," a city humane officer reported.

The lack of supervision and discipline in the home led to an increase in juvenile delinquency in the city. Akron judge Oscar A. Hunsicker said the delinquents were children who were not properly supervised because both parents worked in "vital war industries." Every month seemed to bring larger numbers of truancies, thefts, and runaways. By 1943, the problem was so acute that Judge Hunsicker suggested that the city adopt a curfew and that parents of children who misbehaved be arrested.

In the early days of the war, working mothers who were unable to rely on relatives or hire dependable baby-sitters had little recourse. The Family Service Society was one alternative, but the agency could not handle all the requests. As Margaret Milloy, case supervisor for the Family Service Society, reported, "Requests come in daily for us to care for children of women workers in the factories. Relatives who formerly took care of the youngsters are also appealing for us to take them off their hands." Those children would be placed in one of the one hundred foster homes in the city, "dozens more of these foster homes are needed now, so Family Service Society workers say, as the defense boom grows and more and more mothers are employed," the newspaper reported. Children whose parents worked at Goodyear and Firestone lived in foster homes, but the parents saw them on their off-hours and sometimes took the children home on weekends.

Clearly, in the opening days of World War II, child care options were limited. Nonetheless, more and more mothers with young children were being hired by the rubber companies. More options were needed. The question was what form should they take, who would administer them, and what input—if any—the mothers themselves would have. In Akron, these would be hard questions to answer.

By mid-1942, the city began dealing with the child care issue. Representatives from official quarters—labor, management, education, welfare, and government—met to talk about child care for mothers working in the defense industries. It was, the group agreed, the "worst headache" of war production. The solution that the committee came up with was round-the-clock day care, underwritten by federal funds. In the meantime, mothers had to find their own temporary solutions to their child care problems.

The program at Grace Park provided a temporary solution for the children of mothers who worked first shift. Funded by a government grant, this park offered extended services to preschoolers. There were games and stories during the day, and if it rained, the staff took the three-to-six-year-olds to a nearby community center. This program had tremendous appeal for the families who lived nearby—it was convenient, well supervised, and fun for the children.

The Office of Civilian Defense (OCD) offered another alternative at its East Akron child care facility that opened in the fall of 1942. Open from 6 A.M. to 6 P.M., the facility was designed to serve the mothers who worked the first two shifts—from 6 A.M. to noon and noon to 6 P.M. The center took only children aged two to six and offered supervised play, balanced diets, and rest periods. This facility was widely applauded by the city and became the model for other OCD child care centers. Because of that first facility, as well as the others that soon followed, the Office of Civilian Defense became *the* agency to which working mothers turned. Mary McIntosh, OCD's child care coordinator, began a referral service for mothers who needed child care services. The agency maintained a list of homes willing to take in children. The homes, located throughout the city, had been investigated and approved by social workers. But throughout the war, the OCD had problems getting enough homes to handle the demand. The children placed in these situations often were playmates for sons and daughters in the household. Thus David Seal, two, whose parents worked at Goodyear Aircraft on the first shift, found that he was welcomed into the home of Mr. and Mrs. Richard Noble.

School-age children also needed preschool and after-school activities to keep them out of trouble. (The lack of such facilities was seen as a principal cause of the increased incidence of juvenile delinquency.) In early 1943, a survey conducted by the Akron Board of Education revealed just how great the need was: about fifteen thousand children in Akron were left to shift for themselves while both parents worked. The

Board of Education, however, did not want to get involved in such an enterprise. After defeating such a proposal, the board outlined its objections: there was no immediate need, another group should assume that responsibility, and the program might disrupt homes. It was the failure of the Board of Education to act, however, that seemed to stir the rubber companies and the community to do something.

Rubber companies had never offered child care services; such matters were considered the purview of community organizations. Nonetheless, as absenteeism among women workers climbed and as more mothers entered the workforce, the rubber companies came to see that adequate child care and attendance at work were linked.

Although they did not open day-care centers, the rubber companies got involved in other ways. On a very basic level, the companies helped by scheduling mothers or both parents on the shifts they requested. Goodyear Aircraft, for example, scheduled women workers so children would not be left unsupervised. Dorothy Markle, women's personnel adviser at the company, explained that she helped "countless mothers transfer from one department to another—often with less pay—because the hours are more suitable to family needs." The third shift (10 P.M. to 6 A.M.) was the most popular among mothers with young children. Likewise, rubber companies opened their company newspapers to classified advertising that helped working mothers locate baby-sitters. The companies also surveyed workers to determine the amount and type of child care needs.

Rubber company representatives served on community committees that recommended preschool day care centers and nurseries. The two largest employers of women in the city, Goodyear Tire and Rubber and Goodyear Aircraft, led the way. They enlisted city and county aid, rather than that of the Board of Education, to set up a comprehensive child care program before fall 1943, when large numbers of Akron mothers were expected to be hired. In addition, at least one company, Goodyear Aircraft, listed convenient child care facilities in its company publication and arranged tours of those places.

The negative action by the Board of Education triggered another round of meetings to discuss the child care situation, but again the mothers of the children in question were excluded from these meetings. Instead, representatives of welfare, social, religious, and educational organizations (primarily men) heard Harry Markle, head of the War Manpower Commission in Akron, and Paul Fessenden, a union representative, say that something had to be done to provide child care immediately. The new hiring in the rubber companies had created a demand for round-the-clock care for children aged one to sixteen.

Several agencies dealt with the child care situation. Their solutions ranged from small, community-based efforts to large government-funded programs. The small efforts tended to be led by women. For example, the Girl Scouts offered Tot Lot Playgrounds, afternoon activities for the smallest children. Imitating successful plans in Flint, Dearborn, and Detroit, Girl Scouts—along with their mothers—entertained five or six children in backyards with stories and games and generally kept the tots out of trouble. Although this program had a certain appeal because it was home-based, it still did not fulfill many needs for the mothers who worked because it operated only in the afternoon. Another woman-based program could be found at the Young Woman's Christian Association during the summers. Those services started informally. "That mothers were working and since the children were not in school, the mothers thought the YWCA a good place for their children to 'hang out,' while they were at work," the group's annual report explained.

Religious groups also played a role. The Jewish center began its work in the summer of 1943, caring for seventy-five children in an all-day program and another two hundred in a half-day program. In the summer, the city recreation department expanded its program so children could go to the parks and be kept busy. The most important child care activity, however, was the Metropolitan Housing Authority's centers at the federally financed housing projects. The housing authority worked with the Office of Civilian Defense to develop a child care program that would provide a nurturing environment for the children while their mothers worked. Each center was located near or at the housing projects, but families did not have to live in the projects to use the facilities there. By October 1943, the housing authority had opened four child care centers and planned another six. Early estimates indicated that 245 preschool and 420 school-age children could be handled at these centers. These facilities seemed tailor-made for working mothers. The centers were open from 6 A.M. to 6:30 P.M., which covered the first two production shifts. Several centers expanded their hours. For example, the Wilbeth-Arlington center was open from 5:30 A.M. to 7 P.M. to better accommodate the mothers' schedule and travel to and from work.

Preschoolers stayed all day. School-age children came before and after school. The children who stayed all day were given a well-balanced diet with a hot midday meal, two snacks in the morning and afternoon, and, of course, the requisite daily dose of cod liver oil—all at the low price of fifty cents a day (forty cents for the second child in a family).

Margaret Cooney, who worked at Goodyear Tire and Rubber and lived in the Edgewood projects, remembered those child care facilities well. They were located across the street so it was convenient for Marg-

Day care was a big problem for working mothers with young children. The city attempted to help this situation with its Metropolitan Housing Authority's child care centers at the federally financed housing "projects." Margaret Cooney used the day-care facility in the Edgewood Apartments, where she lived. This picture shows her two children Charles, three, and Sarah, two, in a sandbox at the day-care facility. *Collection of Margaret O'Leary.*

aret to take her two youngsters there. But she used the facilities only to supplement her regular child care arrangements; typically her grandfather took care of the children when she worked. Nonetheless, whenever Margaret needed extra sleep or when her grandfather could not watch the children, she never had any difficulty getting them in to the facility. "They had their meals there and they were well taken care of," Margaret remembered. She was also impressed with their regular activities; the workers "took the children to the park, had games and picnics." They even had birthday parties—"I remember when my daughter was two, they had a party for her" with all the trimmings, even balloons and hats.

Child care was not the only responsibility that married women faced within the home. They also had to do cleaning, cooking, and shopping. Since they worked six days a week, eight hours a day, many mothers had to budget their time carefully to get all their chores done. According to the Women's Bureau, the main desire of women defense workers was to have Saturday off to do laundry and housekeeping. But that never occurred in Akron or its rubber factories.

Early in the war, store hours represented another problem for workers. The stores were open only during the day, which meant that Margaret Cooney, who often worked second or third shift, had to spend her mornings going grocery shopping. She'd pack up her two youngsters and head for the store. "I always had the kids with me. I never went anywhere without them," Margaret explained. But women who worked first shift had little time to get to the store. The situation improved dramatically once the stores and banks in the city changed their hours to accommodate the war workers.

The impetus for this change came from the war workers themselves. Female and male workers had complained that the limited store hours

Shopping represented a problem for women war workers because few stores offered evening hours. By 1942, however, many Akron stores, responding to community pressure, began offering Monday evening hours. This ad for the old Akron Dry Goods store seemed specifically designed to appeal to the woman war worker. Not only was the store open until 9 P.M. on Monday, it also offered a full range of work clothes. Akron Beacon Journal, *August 30, 1942.*

(*Above right*) Transportation sometimes posed a problem for women workers, many of whom did not have a car or could not drive. As this ad asserts, however, the Akron Transportation Company eventually adjusted to the demands. Akron Beacon Journal, *April 15, 1943.*

represented a hardship for them. Many were unable to reach the grocery and department stores until Saturday, if then. In April 1942, the stores, responding to the complaints of the workers, agreed to stay open one night a week—Monday. (The stores were closed Monday morning to accommodate the evening hours.) Akron had been slow to offer evening hours. Stores in Columbus, Dayton, Cincinnati, and Canton already had expanded their hours.

The evening hours met with almost universal acclaim. Women workers had only praise. Rubber worker Anna Dolinsky told a reporter, "For the past two months I haven't been able to shop because of my working hours. I start work at 11 P.M. and I don't have a chance to shop unless I want to lose some sleep." The time she was unable to shop had even been longer for Katherine Strasser, a rubber worker.

Thirty stores, including department, clothing, shoe, millinery, and furniture stores, were in the first wave to adopt expanded hours. But as store managers saw the packed stores on Monday night, others—including the rubber company employee stores—followed suit. Expanding hours seemed to be a smart business decision because Akron war workers had more money to spend than ever before. Women were spotted buying custom-made suits for $150 or paying $39 for a handbag or $15 for a silk necktie for their boyfriends.

The expanded hours helped the city's women workers deal with the wartime shortages, but they did little to help when food shortages hit the city. Women—some of them war workers who took the day off—lined up before stores opened in the hopes of getting meat, coffee, and other items in short supply. In fact, shopping was blamed as one of the principal reasons for absenteeism at the rubber factories even after the stores expanded their hours.

After cooking, shopping, and cleaning, working mothers did not have much time left. Their other activities tended to be child centered. As Margaret Cooney recalled, she spent most of her off-hours with her children. Her favorite destination was Perkins Woods, where the children "could play and I could have a little relaxation." With her husband away at war, Tressie McGee spent most of her off-hours with her daughter, who sang in the church choir and "loved to roller skate." Inez Rogers spent her free time with her three daughters at church. During the war, the church remained a center of the African American community in Akron. Inez and the girls went to church, choir practice, and Bible study.

Several married women whose husbands were in the service had the first great adventures of their lives by going across the country by themselves or with their children. The women who had relatively large disposable incomes often spent their savings to pay for expensive cross-country trips to visit their husbands. Tressie McGee and her daughter took a train to California to visit her husband, who was about to be shipped out. Frances Olechnowicz had no children to take when she went across the country by train to visit her new husband in Seattle. She needed a special month's leave to make the trip. Frances said Goodyear was "pretty nice" about approving those leaves if they were arranged ahead of time.

Married women had precious little time to spend with friends, though they did develop friendships at work. For example, Almeda Bell and her partner at work, Bessie Bellman, had a good deal in common. Both were about the same age and both had children. But their friendship stayed at work. Margaret Cooney never had much time to cultivate her work friendships on her hours off during the war. Only occasionally after getting off work on third shift, at about 6 A.M., did she and a group of two

Married and divorced women who worked in Akron's rubber factories found that they spent much of their free time with their children. Margaret Cooney and Helen Pinto both worked at Goodyear, lived near each other in the projects and took the bus together back and forth to work. The two had something else in common, their children. Here Sally Cooney, Margaret's daughter, and Gary Pinto, Helen's son, play together one sunny afternoon during the war. *Collection of Margaret O'Leary.*

Women followed a certain behavior code during the war. If they were engaged or married, they were expected to stay away from bars and dances; but once their sweethearts were home, they could go out on the town. Here Frances Golliday and her fiance Frank Olechnowicz enjoy some time together before he ships out. *Collection of Frances Olechnowicz.*

or three women stop off for coffee before going home. "I didn't do that very often," she said. "I always figured I had to be home. The kids were little. I said I lived a very dull life when the kids were little." Verna Haag reported similar experiences. She had good friends at Firestone. "We all seemed to have the same thoughts and things and if one person had clothes to exchange that another child could wear, then we'd exchange clothing for children." But outside of work, they never saw these friends. This was another thing that set married women apart from the single female workers at the rubber factories.

Wartime conditions did not necessarily assure matrimonial bliss. During the war, Akron set records in the number of divorces filed and granted. Common Pleas Court judge Oscar A. Hunsicker gave war prosperity as the reason for the high divorce rates. Wives who had been unhappy in their marriages before the war could now afford to divorce their spouses. "There seems to be no question that many couples who lived together in depression years are now taking advantage of their new-found prosperity to separate," the judge explained. "Wives who lived with their husbands merely because they couldn't afford a divorce now have jobs."

But the situation was not as simple as Judge Hunsicker implied. Depression-era marital unhappiness did not explain all the divorces during wartime and immediately after. Conditions at work exacerbated the situation. Some married women found new romances at work. As Thelma Bolen observed, she kept herself apart from many of her co-workers at Firestone particularly for that reason. "I never became friendly with people at Firestone because . . . everybody was cheating on everybody. And I was married at the time and I just didn't become too friendly. I wouldn't go to anything that I was invited to," she explained.

By 1944, the divorce rate was twice as high as it had been ten years before. Married women rushed to the courts in what was termed the "greatest tidal wave of divorce suits in the history of Summit County." Clerk of Courts Verne C. Bender said that a new divorce record was established almost every week. In the fiscal year that ended July 30, 1944, 2,540 divorce petitions were filed and 1,605 were granted, compared to 1,298 petitions in 1934 and 805 divorces granted in 1934. Women most commonly received divorces on the grounds of gross neglect and extreme cruelty, according to the news reports of the day.

A large number of married working women, especially those with children, faced a restricted lifestyle in wartime Akron. In contrast, single women discovered that Akron offered all kinds of new sights, sounds, and experiences. With more money than they had ever earned before and with new friends, many women workers went out to discover all that Akron had to offer. Some of the lures were not socially acceptable, but many women workers set out to experience them anyway, comfortable in the anonymity that the big city of Akron afforded them.

Friendships were often first forged during training. Isabel Moran met her friend Jean Haig at training school for Firestone. Jean was a few years older than Isabel, who had just turned eighteen in 1943, but the two seemed to hit it off. They did everything together—from working as partners in the factory wiring planes to going out on the town. They went to movies, ate out, and shopped together. They were both engaged so the dances, so popular with the women workers, were off limits. Sometimes, they just went over to each other's houses; both women lived with their parents.

When Billie and Ruth Schott, who were cousins, moved into the YWCA in Akron in the hopes of getting a job at Goodyear Aircraft, they did not know a soul in the city. That was soon remedied at Goodyear's training school. The two met a circle of friends that would last through the war and after. They met Irma Garrett of Stow, Elsie Bucholtz of Massillon, Bea Gillian of Pennsylvania, and Betty Francis of Akron. The women worked together, played together, and soon lived together. All worked in the same department; all worked the same day shift. Thus it only seemed natural that the six would move in together. Initially they rented a cottage on Portage Lakes; but once the summer was over, they rented a house—and a car. Elsie was the only one who knew how to drive so she was the chauffeur. The six often dressed alike and went to dances and nightclubs together; sometimes they told the gullible that they were

Friendships between women did not stop at the factory gates. Women, especially the single women, lived and played together after work as well. Here Greta Sligert (left) and Dolly Bell pause on their way to B. F. Goodrich. The two were close friends who often went to dances and movies together. *Collection of Dolly Bell Romito.*

singers for the popular orchestra leader Tommy Dorsey. They also went to bars; Billie Schott met her husband-to-be at Detz's, a bar on Portage Lake. But most of the time they just had fun at home—playing cards, short-sheeting beds, or doing some "crazy things," Billie explained.

Dorothy Chevin had her friend Eleanor Bailey to thank for introducing her to her future husband. Dorothy and Eleanor worked together at Goodyear and met shortly after Dorothy had moved from Cleveland to work at Goodyear. Eleanor was from Garrettsville. The two worked in the same department and "just hit it off." They went to movies and shopping after work. When Eleanor's brother was home on leave, she introduced him to Dorothy. They were soon dating and eventually got married.

Thelma Moore, just eighteen when she got her job at Goodyear Aircraft, met her friends Mac and Mary, who came from West Virginia together and roomed together, on the job. Thelma had no West Virginia connection, but nonetheless the three became inseparable. They seemed to have a good deal in common: they were about the same age and each had a romantic interest in the service. Mac had a boyfriend, Mary had a husband, and Thelma married her boyfriend while working at Goodyear. Mary and Mac were much more worldly wise than Thelma. Both drank; Thelma did not, which became quite apparent one evening when the three went out to celebrate. Thelma got sick and threw up all over the car that Mac and Mary had borrowed. Afraid that if Thelma returned home in that condition she would lose her place, the others took her to their apartment to get her sober. The three also once went to a "girlie show" together. They never expected the lights to come on, but when they did, Thelma recalled, "We were all embarrassed. We grabbed our coats and flew out of there."

Drinking among women—and especially women workers—became so widespread that the newspaper began reporting about the "barroom sirens" who frequented the city's saloons. Typically the women came in pairs, making the "rounds of the town's hot spots." The largest number of them appeared to be women war workers who had "too much money in their pockets and too few places to spend it," the newspaper observed. But as one woman explained, the answer was not that simple. Women needed each other's companionship in this time of war. Bars were just convenient places to go. She explained, "Of course, women are drinking more. . . . The men are all away and they [women] naturally go out together to keep themselves happy and cheerful. They feel the need of being together more in war times, when their men are away."

Many women, especially the young workers, went out drinking on the weekends. Grace Hanlon explained that she and many friends would go out "and drink beer [and] dance." Typically these were single women, but sometimes married women would join them. Bars and nightclubs were convenient places to go to unwind. They offered refreshments, food, and good music. But that entertainment was expensive. As Grace recalled, "[we] didn't go out often; [we] didn't have the money. Money came hard back in them days."

"Hundreds" of Goodyear Aircraft women smoked. It is not clear if these women smoked before the war or if they picked up the habit at work, but smoking was widespread among the women who worked in the rubber factories. When tobacco got more difficult to obtain in cigarette form, some of these women switched from "fags" to pipes.

(*Opposite*) When Billie Schott moved to Akron to work at Goodyear Aircraft, she knew only one other person, her cousin Ruth. But that was quickly remedied. During training, she met a circle of friends that she would live with, play with, and laugh with. They are Ruth Schott, Marion Salbany, Betty Francis, Billie Schott, Beatrice Elaine Gillen, Irma M. Jarrett, and Elsie Bucholtz. Six of the seven lived together in a house—with only one bathroom. The seven also liked to dress alike; they would tell the gullible they were singers for the popular orchestra leader Tommy Dorsey. *Collection of Billie Cardarelli.*

Even though women worked eight hours a day, six days a week, they—especially young, single women—went out and had fun. In the summer, the place to go was the beach. Here Grace Hanlon (right), who worked at Goodyear, enjoys a day at Edgewater Park with a friend from Cleveland. *Collection of Grace Fannin.*

(*Opposite, top left*) The city's theaters also adjusted to the war workers' schedules as this advertisement in the *Beacon Journal* suggests. In 1943, the Strand offered a thirty-two-hour continuous show of the movie *Air Force*. Workers were invited to come after any shift "DRESSED AS YOU ARE AND SEE A COMPLETE SHOW ANY TIME THROUGHOUT THE NIGHT." Akron Beacon Journal, *April 21, 1943.*

(*Opposite, bottom left*) The women workers loved to dance, and Akron was the home of many ballrooms that featured live orchestras. This ad for the Hawaiian Room at the Mayflower Hotel featured Gardner Benedict and his orchestra. The East Market Gardens was a favorite among the women rubber workers. Akron Beacon Journal, *April 19, 1943.*

This is not to say that all the single women who worked in the rubber factories during World War II were out and about, drinking, and smoking. More went to the movies, to the dances, or to grab a "bite" after work. The newspapers merely focused on the women who smoked and drank and played a role in the "rootin', tootin'" good times on Saturday night in the big city of Akron. The only thing these single women needed was money (something they usually had plenty of) and energy (something that was in short supply). Leona Smarr remembered that she often did not have a lot of energy after work. "I'd eat, listen to radio news to see how the war was progressing, go to bed."

A problem shared by both the single and married women workers was the serious housing shortage in the city. Women from outside the Akron metropolitan area who were recruited by the companies already had places to stay because government guidelines required the rubber companies to find suitable accommodations for people they recruited from out of town. The corporations were fairly efficient in locating housing for these women. The companies either queried their own workers about available rooms in their households or they plugged into the information obtained in a survey of households in Summit County. In 1942, at the same time that the War Manpower Commission canvassed households in Summit county for men and women available for war work, the agency also asked about the number of rooms available to

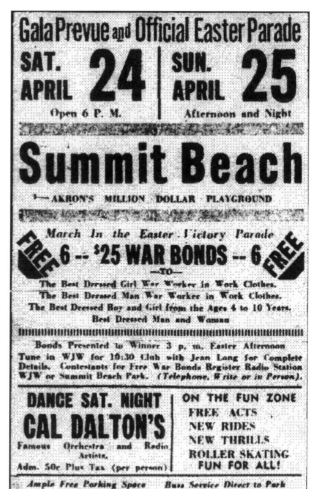

rent to war workers coming into the city. Elmer Kaufman of the housing bureau explained that he kept a list of hundreds of rooms available for men and women. Kaufman carried his list day and night, never sure when a busload of new recruits would arrive at the terminal.

Akron families were encouraged to take in "war production guests" or rent spare bedrooms to war workers. Single women workers typically relied on sleeping rooms in private households, which usually meant that the women enjoyed clean, safe living arrangements in a supervised setting. Thelma Bolen was only eighteen when she took a room with a family on Sherman Street, but when she got into a fight at work and returned to the house disheveled, she was given a week to move out. The owners told her, "'We're a Christian home. We don't believe in women doing that.' They didn't give me a chance to explain. They just told me I had to move," Thelma remembered. As it turned out, that probably was the best thing for her. She moved in with the Johnsons on East Thornton Street in a sleeping room that did not include meals. But

(*Above*) Summit Beach Park was one of the playgrounds of the city. And it, like so many other of Akron's attractions, adjusted to war and the demands of the war workers. Here, the park offers a range of options for war workers Easter weekend 1943. The Easter Victory Parade offered prizes (war bonds) to the "Best Dressed Girl War Worker in Work Clothes" and the "Best Dressed Man War Worker in Work Clothes" among others. Saturday night, the park planned a dance with Cal Dalton's "Famous Orchestra." Akron Beacon Journal, *April 21, 1943.*

Many companies organized concerts and other activities for the war workers. This concert, held on July 13, 1944, at the Akron Rubber Bowl, featured Harry James and his band, with Morton Downey. The concert was sponsored by the Akron Coca-Cola Bottling Company and the Akron Industry, Labor, and Civil Defense group. *Collection of Kathleen Endres.*

(*Opposite*) During the war, Mildred Zelei worked during the day for Sun Rubber making gas masks but on weekends she was a pilot for the Civil Air Patrol in Akron. Here she poses by a CJ3 that she flew at the old Ling Field. Mildred started at Sun Rubber right after she graduated from Norton High School in 1938. She "borrowed" her sister's birth certificate to get that job because Sun Rubber would not hire anyone under the age of twenty-one. Mildred was only seventeen at the time. In the late 1930s, Mildred made the toys for which Sun Rubber was so famous. When the Sun factory shifted to war production, she made gas masks. Mildred was active in the URW local at Sun. She was secretary of the local and a three-time delegate to the URW conventions. During the war, she was the only woman on Summit County's War Manpower Commission. In 1944, following the death of her brother Stephen in France, Mildred left Sun Rubber and joined the Women's Air Corps. *Collection of Mildred Eakin.*

soon the Johnsons began to look after Thelma as a daughter. When Thelma was too tired to eat out, the Johnsons insisted that she eat with them and refused to accept any money. Thelma's experiences illustrated possibilities for the women. The household owner could exercise a control over the renter's behavior, but the owner could also display a nurturing environment such as the one Thelma found so appealing with the Johnsons.

Some women workers preferred to live with one another. Eleanor Bailey and Dorothy Chevin decided to move in together after they had developed a close friendship at work at Goodyear. Agnes Lackney found that living with Stella Bennett, her friend from Firestone, benefited both of them financially. Stella, whose husband was in the navy, had two daughters. She asked Agnes if she'd like to move in. The two women and the two children lived together until Stella's husband returned from the service.

Sometimes a larger number of buddies from work opted to live together. That turned out to be a positive experience for Billie Schott, her cousin, and four friends who worked together at Goodyear Aircraft. The six pooled their resources and were able to rent a furnished house in 1943. "It was amazing how well we got along. We didn't have any fights or anything. We just worked things out," Billie remembered.

Not all women were as lucky in their living accommodations. Some women who lived together found that they had to rent converted buildings. Dorothy Chevin remembered one group of Goodyear workers that rented a converted beauty saloon where five women lived. Each stall became a bedroom with a bed and a set of drawers. One bathroom served all five women.

Working mothers had the most difficult time finding housing. Single-family houses were in short supply and some owners did not allow children. Other rental properties were not fit to live in. Women with

WANTED!
ANY VACANCY

FOR WAR
WORKERS

Furnished Or Unfurnished
Houses Or Apartments

Light Housekeeping Rooms
Or
Sleeping Rooms

No Commission
Charged

Employes' Housing
Goodyear Aircraft Corp.

Call Mr. Berry
FR-1471, Ext. 8154

Call 8 a. m. To 5 p. m.

Akron faced a chronic housing shortage. When the rubber companies recruited from outside the area, they needed to provide housing for these workers. The rubber companies located some of that housing by advertising in the city's newspaper. Here Goodyear Aircraft searches for unfurnished houses, apartments, or sleeping rooms. Akron Beacon Journal, *April 21, 1942.*

During the war, Olga Cikowich shared an apartment with her cousin, who also worked at Goodyear. *Collection of Sandra Mondrich.*

children often found that converted store buildings could serve as new homes. Mary Lucille Young, her sister Elizabeth Harper, and her two children thought a converted gas station was ideal. "It's lots nicer to live in a gas station than in a crowded old rooming house," Elizabeth explained.

Another way Akron dealt with the housing shortage was with mobile housing. Beginning in 1942, more and more trailers were used to house families. Gertrude Jewell, for example, moved her family from Zanesville so she could work at Goodyear Aircraft. She and her two children eventually found housing in a trailer on Massillon Road. The trailers, however, were not always welcomed into neighborhoods. In 1943, the newspaper reported that residents of the tenth ward organized to oppose the portable housing proposed for their community.

The projects alleviated Akron's housing problem temporarily. The first, Edgewood Homes, was located on Cole Avenue and was designed specifically to house war workers. Margaret Cooney was one of the working mothers who moved into that facility. She remembered, "At that time those apartments were brand new and they had baby-sitting facilities across the street." But the projects did not solve the housing shortage for long. By 1943, public housing officials were reporting that their offices were swamped with requests for dwellings, apartments, and light housekeeping rooms. Throughout much of the war, housing remained a major problem that the rubber companies, the city of Akron, and the various federal agencies could never fully solve. Indeed, it was frequently cited as one of the reasons why the city could not recruit or retain skilled workers.

Single and married women rubber workers also shared equal access to planned corporate, union, and community-based activities. Goodyear Tire and Rubber, Goodyear Aircraft, Goodrich, and Firestone sponsored a wide range of clubs designed to appeal to women workers. Most of these activities were gender-based; often they were sports-related. Recreation directors organized the activities, and each gender had its own director. At Firestone the recreation director for women was Dorothy Minto. At Goodyear, that position was held by Rosemary Anderson. Baseball, basketball, swimming, and bowling were the most popular female sports activities.

Young female Goodyear Aircraft workers liked having a good time. Here nine Goodyear Aircraft workers enjoy the afternoon sun at a cottage at Portage Lakes. The women are Ruth Schott, Bea Gillian, Elsie Buchholtz, Billie Schott, Irma Gerrit, Martha Riski, Elizabeth Riski and an unidentified woman. *Collection of Billie Cardarelli.*

Rubber companies also offered clubs that were designed for self-improvement. Goodyear offered a Personality Club, to improve "personaltiy [*sic*], learning the art of smart conversation, grammar, posture, grooming, etiquette." Goodyear also offered physical fitness classes for women employees and their families. In 1945, forty-five women participated in the opening class of the second series of women's conditioning classes at the Goodyear gym. Goodrich offered cultural opportunities through its Girls Silvertown Orchestra. More than thirty Goodrich women played in that orchestra.

It is unclear what categories of women participated in these activities. Team and league time requirements probably limited the involvement of married women in many of the team sports. Several corporate-sponsored activities, however, did lend themselves to involving married women, especially women with children. For example, the annual company picnics were ideal outings for married women and their children. The company-sponsored Christmas activities that featured children's visits to Santa drew the married woman worker and her family. Victory gardens on company-donated plots also attracted married women and their children.

Women themselves organized some activities, which tended to share certain characteristics: they seldom required a long-term commitment of time, they involved only a small number of women, and they had an air of informality. Betty Demitri's spaghetti dinner for eight Firestone women inspectors from the clean-up and miscellaneous department was

Sunbathing was always a way to pass the time, even during wartime. Goodyear opened its roof so women—and men—could take in the rays at lunchtime. Women laid out on Tuesday and Thursday, men on Monday, Wednesday, and Friday. Here Edith Mowery applies suntan lotion to Helen Auler. *Goodyear Collection.*

typical, as was the "sunbathing" on top of Goodyear Hall. Both were quickly organized. Neither required a major commitment of time.

Rarer—but better publicized—were the large events staged and organized by women in specific departments. But even these did not demand a long-term commitment of time. Goodyear's gas mask department, primarily females, sponsored a dance at the German American Club in June 1942. Almost four hundred people attended the dance that raised $152 for the USO. These formal activities organized by women were the exception. Far more common were smaller, informal get-togethers, easily and quickly organized.

Women sometimes initiated community activities, but not always with the expected, pleasant results. For example, three women workers from Goodyear Aircraft, Lois Reis, Mildred Reed, and Anne Jenkins, were responsible for setting up special activities for women who worked second shift. The three went to the YWCA saying that women of the second shift had little to do outside of work; and they wanted the Y to set up

On top of Goodyear Hall, Marjorie Casey, Virginia Bobes, Nancy McAdams, Betty Leonard, Edith Mowery, Mildred Bangham, Helen Auler, Gertrude Sams, and Louise Ziegenhiem spend their lunch hour sunbathing. *Goodyear Collection.*

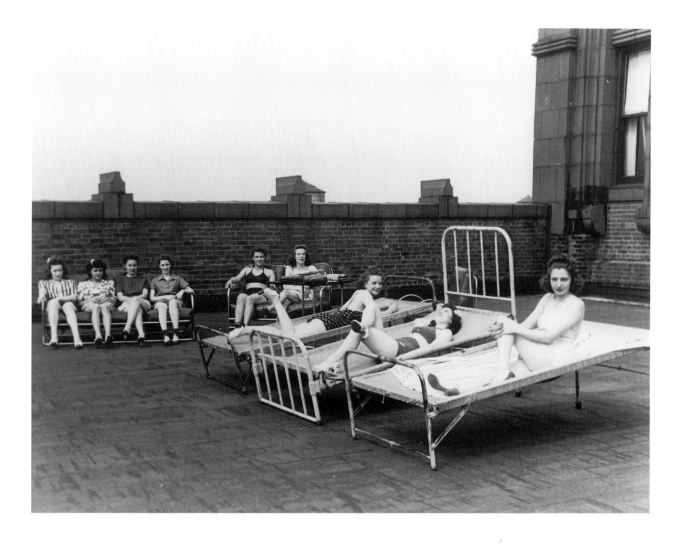

During the war, one of the favorite pastimes for young women was dancing, and one of the favorite places for women rubber workers to do their dancing was East Market Gardens. Here Gladys, a BFG employee, and James Gibson pose after a dance at East Market Gardens. This was taken at one of the so-called colored dances held at the ballroom. *Collection of Gladys Gibson.*

some activities. The YWCA agreed to come up with a program of sports and fitness but required participants to pass physicals. Six of the women failed their physicals. "Two of the girls did not take this failure graciously and caused a disturbance, demanding their money back," the YWCA annual report explained. Notwithstanding the disturbance, the Y did attempt to pursue these programs, but with little success. The group had much more success in its programs that were offered to first- and third-shift workers. Again, these were impromptu and did not demand a large commitment of time. Women were merely invited to use the Y, adjacent to Goodyear Plant One, for "an hour or two of relaxation," free of charge. It is unclear how many women—married or single—were able to find "an hour or two" for relaxation.

Goodrich's URW Local aimed its dances at the young singles. The dances were scheduled to start at 7 A.M., right after the third shift ended. Workers normally made their dates at the factory and then headed for the dance.

The companies, the union, and the community, then, attempted to provide socially acceptable off-hour activities for the women workers. But these activities were not the only alternatives in the city of Akron. As women workers—especially single women—soon discovered, there was a wide range of options open to them, from dances at the East Market Gardens to drinking at the nightclubs of the city. Recreation, of course, was not the only thing that filled the off-hours of these women. Working mothers still had to carry on their traditional household and child care responsibilities—even after working eight hours a day, six days a week—and had little time for relaxation.

Although balancing house, family, and job was difficult, the working mothers were not always ready to give up their high wages and their factory work once the rubber companies began converting back to peace-time production. Likewise, single women rubber workers, who were used to the lifestyle their big weekly paychecks financed, were not always ready to go back to their badly paid, "nonessential" jobs.

six

The Conversion of Rosie

Agnes Lackney and Isabel Moran probably never met each other during World War II. Nonetheless, they had much in common. They were from small towns in Ohio: Agnes from Byesville and Isabel from Sycamore. Both had moved up to Akron before the war: Agnes with her sister in 1937, Isabel with her mother in 1940. Both quickly found work: Agnes doing domestic work, Isabel as the popcorn girl at Scot's downtown. Both went to work at Firestone during World War II: Agnes in 1941, Isabel in 1943. But there the similarities end. Agnes worked for Firestone Tire and Rubber making one-man boats, life belts, pontoons, and parts for Bofors guns during the war. Isabel got her job in Firestone's burgeoning Aviation Products Division. She worked on final assembly wings. It was a great job that she enjoyed.

Agnes still remembers the end of the war: "My God, everybody dropped their tools and out the door they went. You'd thought there was a fire. Jumped in the cars, driving up and down Main Street, honking their horns and running into bars. Nobody said good-bye or anything. They just shot out the door to celebrate and that was the end of all those people's jobs." But Agnes was lucky. "I was number 27 on the [seniority] list. They kept 27 women. I was number 27. But the other girls never got called back. They had less service than me." Agnes stayed at Firestone another thirty years, retiring at the age of fifty-seven.

Isabel was not as lucky. After celebrating V-E Day, Isabel went back to work. "We went to work and they said we're closing down." She wanted to continue work, but Firestone told her to report for unemployment—

and she did, once. "I went one time and I couldn't stand sitting around, not having something to do. So I got a job at . . . one of the places downtown. And I didn't like that very well so I wasn't there very long." Isabel never went back to Firestone or applied at another rubber company. She started a new life instead, as a wife and mother.

Agnes Lackney and Isabel Moran illustrate the range of alternatives for the women rubber workers after the war. Some remained in the rubber factories, retiring after decades of service. Others found they no longer had a job and left regretfully.

Others were like Dolly Bell, who worked at Goodrich. She had been on the job for only about a year when the war ended. Nonetheless, she had enough seniority to stay on and did until 1950, when she married. "I really wanted to work," Dolly remembered, "but my husband didn't want me to work" so she left the factory. In contrast, Betty Pinter never intended to keep her job at Goodrich after the war. She finished her shift on V-J Day "and told my boss good-bye and I quit."

The women and men in BFG's bullet-proof fuel-tank production take time off to celebrate a victory by the Allies. *B. F. Goodrich Collection.*

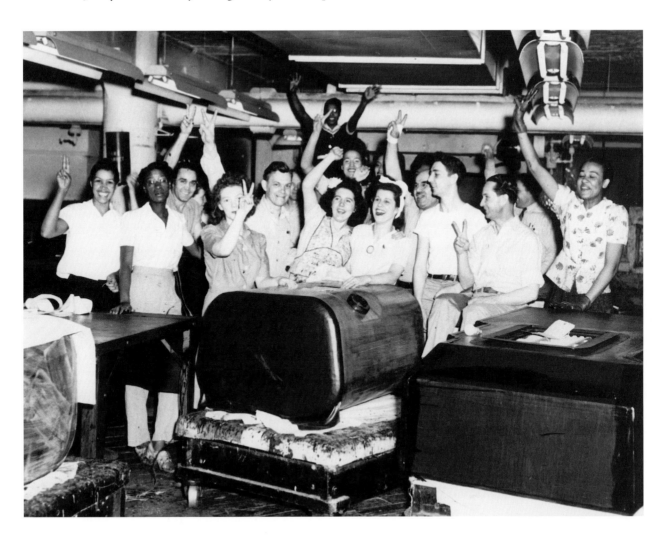

The men and women at Goodyear Aircraft celebrate when hearing the news of the bombing of Tokyo by B-29 Super Fortresses. This picture was taken in the section of the plant where bomb bay and tail surfaces were produced. *Goodyear Collection.*

The conversion of Rosie the Rubber Worker to peacetime is a complicated tale, not unlike but also different from the story of women workers in other wartime occupations. Because of conditions unique to the Akron area, the rubber industry did not simply convert from wartime to peacetime production. As early as 1943, the companies began transferring war production—much of it done by women—out of the city. The conversion that followed the war was merely the largest of the series. Many women (and fewer men) were laid off after the war, but there were fewer reductions because of those prewar conversions.

The rubber industry continued to need women production workers after the war. The conversion to peacetime products in the rubber industry did not just mean increased manufacture of tires, a product line traditionally associated with male labor. It also meant a host of peacetime products, like garden hoses, tubes, hot water bottles, toys, and many other, smaller items more commonly associated with female production.

The rubber companies began the wartime conversions because of the chronic labor shortages in the city. The conversion process began in 1943. The largest rubber companies, which were also the largest employers of women, were the ones most active in shifting wartime production out of the city. Those other locations were typically smaller cities in Ohio or in the South—locations that did not have the chronic labor shortage that plagued Akron throughout much of the war. General moved a large part of its life-belt manufacturing to Columbiana, Ohio. Seiberling shipped some of its rubber boat and pontoon production to Wooster, Ohio, and its molded goods production to small plants in southern Ohio. Firestone transferred fuel cell production to three other plants outside Akron and its flotation gear department to Winston-Salem, North Carolina. Bᴀ diffused its deicer and fuel cell manufacturing to five other plants.

The largest number of these products had been manufactured by women. The women who were thus displaced did not necessarily lose

Bꜰɢ women workers celebrate V-E Day outside the men's factory employment office. *B. F. Goodrich Collection.*

their jobs. Many were shifted into other departments or joined other war production facilities; others simply left production work altogether. A reporter for the *Beacon Journal* saw the relocation as a positive development: "This reconversion in Akron's basic rubber production is placing the city in the forefront of the industrial parade back to peacetime goods." That shift meant that more time, energy, machinery, and factory space could be devoted to tire production, traditionally the job of "husky males." But in 1944, women had been introduced into that production process. These women had taken over men's jobs in whole or in part.

The conversions of 1943 and 1944 forced some women production workers to leave the rubber industry well before the end of the war. The number of women working in the rubber factories, for example, had gone from 23,635 in November 1943, when the first conversion was widely publicized, to 17,775 in May 1945. In the aircraft industry, the number of women went from 13,738 in November 1943 to 9,645 in May 1945. What happened to those 10,000 displaced women was not entirely clear. Harry Markle, head of the area War Manpower Commission, speculated, "A good many of them, especially the local women, went back home—content to drop out of war employment when they were no longer needed . . . others have gone back to their hometowns—or to new jobs in other areas."

At the same time rubber companies were shifting production out of the city, those same corporations, the city of Akron, and the union began planning for the postwar period. Representatives from industry, business, labor, civic, and educational groups met to consider plans. The Committee for Economic Development did surveys and weighed the factors that would affect the city's future—and all the reports seemed to say the same thing: Akron and the rubber industry should have no difficulty making the transition from a wartime economy to a peacetime one. Surveys indicated that employers—and especially the rubber companies—expected to have more employees in the postwar period than in the immediate prewar year. All agreed that the city's employers could not be expected to keep up their peak war employment—layoffs had to come, especially once the veterans returned. But the city of Akron and the rubber companies would be in much better shape than most cities or industries. The demand for tires was expected to keep the factories running, and the women and men still making fuel cells, pontoons, and other military products could be reassigned to making rubber parts for new autos or one of "hundreds of other civilian items." No one predicted any extreme postwar unemployment in the rubber industry.

Just how many women would be needed to meet peacetime production needs was a concern that led the United Rubber Workers national union to adopt the resolution, "That everything possible shall be done to protect the economic positions of women members; that they should be guaranteed continued employment on the basis of seniority." Nonetheless, in an industry committed to the seniority system, women and African Americans who had been hired during the war could not always be assured of job security, no matter how much planning took place.

Women who had jobs in the rubber factories before the war could expect to keep them after the war. As a Department of Labor report observed, "Women who had pre-war jobs in the rubber industry will return to those jobs after the war with their accumulated company service credit. Women as well as Negroes who entered the rubber industry for the first time during the war production period, are at the bottom of the seniority lists, and if production is curtailed, they will have no real job protection."

That prediction, however, did not necessarily come to pass. Beginning with V-E Day, factories began laying off workers—especially women. Dorothy F. Markle thought that the women would welcome the change: "What will these women do after the war? With the exception of those who have to work, most of them will be glad to go home. Their post-war plans are very simple: they want to go home to their men and children. They will be happy to trade their drills and micrometers for a vacuum cleaner and a sewing machine. They are tired, and they are feeling the tension of 'war nerves.'"

Frances Perkins, secretary of labor, predicted that women workers would marry the returning soldiers, give up their jobs, and stay home. "As a matter of fact, nature will take care of that problem [women remaining in the factories after the war] as 90 percent of our women want to live in homes and have families."

Some of the women workers echoed that expectation—at least those were the ones quoted in newspapers. For example, Mildred Wilcox, who worked in Goodyear's tube room, looked forward to the return of her two sons, Thomas and Donald, from the war. She told a *Beacon* reporter, "I'm staying on my job until the war is won and my boys come home again. Then I'm going to spend all my time cooking and keeping house." Similarly, the Summit County Committee for Economic Development predicted that women who were laid off would either return to their hometowns, go back to school, or return to housekeeping.

The largest number of women laid off after V-E and V-J Day in Akron had been employed in aircraft production at Firestone Aviation

Products and Goodyear Aircraft. These two manufacturing divisions had been especially hard hit by the $100 million in canceled government contracts. Dorothy Watson had worked at Firestone in the anodizing department, where she stamped airplane parts with a number and put a stripe on airplane panels. She remembered, "When I entered the plant [on V-E Day], it was quiet as a tomb. All the machinery had been turned off. Employees were standing around laughing. After a while, we were told to go home. The war was over. That was the last day of work." That was a common experience at Firestone Aviation Products. By August 1945, almost all of Firestone Aviation's business had been canceled. Most of the workers—including large numbers of women—were laid off. Between the wing panel operations and the gun mount division, almost five thousand workers, primarily women, lost their jobs.

Edith "Whitey" White Franks found a similar situation at Goodyear Aircraft. "I worked there at D3 plant for about three years. I bought, each week, a 'war bond,' as we called them. I went to school on the third floor, worked on final assembly till the war ended. What a great celebration. A group of friends and myself stole as much toilet paper as we could get out past the gatehouse, decorated our cars, then drove downtown Akron tooting horns and acting like 'wild people.' Next day we went back to work to check in 'company' tools and got our own tool boxes and that was the end of it," she wrote in the *Beacon* years later.

In August 1945, Goodyear Aircraft announced plans to lay off fifteen thousand of its eighteen thousand employees. The layoffs were to come swiftly, at a rate of fifteen hundred per day. Most of those workers were women. P. W. Litchfield, chairman of Goodyear, explained that with the end of the war, armament, shipbuilding, and aircraft production would be significantly cut back. He told the employees: "Goodyear Aircraft must therefore demobilize, with keen regret that our organization must shrink to a small fraction of its wartime size, that the buddies working beside us must be scattered and find new connections. To some it will mean a welcome relief, by going back to their homes and families, to others a need to start over again somewhere else. To those who remain will fall the task of building peacetime products in a competitive market with all the assistance that Goodyear can give."

Ada Phillips welcomed that news. She told a reporter for the company newspaper, "I've never been so happy. This is what we have been working for and now that it has finally come I'm so glad to get back to my home again." Martha Neff, who had two sons in the service, explained, "Home is where I want to be now." Grace Johnson was going to go back to Hickory, North Carolina, to see her husband. All the women quoted in the company newspaper emphasized that they were happy to be returning to their homes.

Some of the pressure was reduced when women, like Betty Pinter, voluntarily left the workforce after the war ended. Other options were offered. At BFG's Mill Four, Industrial Products, and Aeronautical Divisions, women could accept a voluntary sixty-day leave of absence and then come back. If they refused to accept the leave, they would be removed from the rolls. Most of the women workers in the rubber and tire factories were saved when the Akron rubber companies agreed to revert to the thirty-six-hour workweek, from the forty-eight-hour standard. That move virtually eliminated the need for layoffs.

The end of the war also brought a reshuffling of the female labor force. Union and company agreements prevented women from keeping higher-paying men's jobs once male workers were again available. Those women returned to jobs traditionally done by women, like making drug and surgical sundries, auto parts, V-belts, bike tires, and a host of smaller products. Or as a Department of Labor report explained, "Now, as before the war, the departments engaged in assembling, testing, and curing the inflated rubber products employ chiefly women. The only change is that since the manpower shortage mechanical adjustments have been made in the machines, and many of the heavier jobs formerly done by men have been broken down into lighter, relatively simple operations."

Thus, Agnes Lackney shifted from making parts for the Bofors guns to the Plant Two tire room, making juvenile tires, a job done by women before the war. She opted for a brief, voluntary lay-off instead—a kind of three-week "vacation." When she returned, she went to work in the tire room. Although Dolly Bell had only about a year's seniority when the war ended, that was enough for her to stay on at BFG. But self-sealing tanks were not in her future. At first, she worked in the department making golf balls, but she was bumped by someone with more seniority. Then she went on to buffing, but the machine was too big for her to handle. After complaining to personnel, she was transferred to the department making lifeboats for ships. She stayed on that job until 1950, when she married and quit.

Some women found that they were no longer supervisors. Frances Olechnowicz had been a supervisor in the gas mask department; after the war, that department no longer existed and neither did her job. She went on to piecework as a splicer, which was not an easy transition. She reported that she was harassed on the job, that sometimes the men would play jokes on her and once put a dead mouse under the fabric she was working with.

Ernestine and Frank Rogers enjoy some moments together before he was shipped out. Ernestine had come up from West Virginia to work at Goodyear Aircraft before her marriage. She quit to be with her new husband. In 1944, she moved back to Akron to work at Goodrich's Miller Plant. After the war, she was laid off, but she had no plans to continue to work at Goodrich anyway. *Collection of Ernestine Rogers.*

Laid-off production workers—the largest number of whom were women from the aviation manufacturing facilities in the city—reported to the U.S. Employment Service in hope of finding other jobs, and they applied for unemployment. But when they reported to the USES, they found few jobs for women. The 5,492 female former war workers drawing unemployment in October 1945 had to compete for only three hundred jobs for women. In contrast, the USES could not fill the six thousand jobs for "trained, husky men," as tire builders. Women were not considered for those positions, even though during the war, hundreds of women had been trained to do just that work.

The rubber companies requesting women workers were merely replacing women who had left. They did not see their former women workers as realistic applicants for many of the new positions in the peacetime plants. The laid-off workers "are not always qualified to be transferred to the kind of operations that we are now engaged in," BFG president John L. Collyer said in a radio broadcast. Women, who had done tire building during the war, were no longer considered qualified to do it after the war. Instead, the rubber companies sent recruiters throughout Ohio, Pennsylvania, West Virginia, Kentucky, and Indiana looking for men to handle the heavy work and hung posters in army separation centers throughout the Midwest telling about job opportunities in Akron.

By late 1945, newspaper reporters proclaimed the rubber industry "reconverted." An estimated 28,000 women still held jobs in February 1946, a slight increase over 1940, when 27,400 women worked in Summit County. These figures leave the impression that the number of wom-

Many women were laid off after the war, but they were not driven out of the rubber factories. Certain types of training remained open to women after the war. In 1951, for example, these women graduated from Goodyear's women's drafting class. *Front:* Jacqueline Brannon, Theresa Heffernan, Helen Walters, Doris Huffman, Jeanne La Rue, Edith Seabolt, Dorothy Lockhart, Nada Thomas, Agnes Karon. *Back:* Dolores Vronick, Patricia Spring, Lois Worrell, Nancy Martin, Carolyn Cochran, Nina Whatley, Claire McLaughlin, Beverly Weinberg, Ann Simek, Betty Gorbe, Beverly Housley. *Goodyear Collection.*

en in the rubber industry had returned to prewar levels, but that is not the case. The percentage of women in the postwar labor force in the rubber industry was actually below prewar levels. In 1940, women represented 25.4 percent of the rubber industry workforce. In 1946, after the rubber industry had been declared reconverted, that percentage had dropped to 24.3. Only in 1920 had women represented a smaller portion of the rubber industry workforce, according to census reports.

Women who returned to the lower-paying jobs in the industry made about two-thirds what the men made. That they accepted these low-paying jobs may actually have protected the women. By January 1946, the rubber factories had reached their labor saturation point for both men and women. Yet veterans, most without rubber industry reemployment rights, were returning to Akron. As one union official explained, "Most G.I.'s couldn't afford to take one of these low-paying jobs." The gender segmentation had been reimposed in the rubber factories.

Within the confines of this gender segmentation, however, women rubber workers would increase their presence in the rubber industry. By 1950, women workers represented 27 percent of the total workforce in the rubber industry, according to Labor Department statistics. The increased percentage did not mean a change in the character of the work environment itself but did reflect the desire on the part of the women of Akron and other cities to earn the high wages offered by the rubber industry.

The war had left its mark on the city. The "projects" would remain a long-standing testament to the housing shortages of wartime Akron. The women workers who had saved their money to pay for a home would spur a new phase of construction in the city and in the suburbs. Retailing would never be quite the same, as grocery, department, and specialty shops continued their evening hours—at least once a week. Yet other stores, including Sears, preferred the prewar patterns without a night option.

So how closely did Rosie in the rubber factory resemble Rosie of the posters? Some mirrored the stereotype. They came to Akron's rubber factories without previous work experience, had been motivated only by patriotic considerations, and planned to leave the workforce as soon as the war ended. A larger number varied considerably from that picture. Most of the women rubber workers during the war came from working-class traditions and had been employed before the war, either in industry or in service occupations. Those who had never been employed were usually young girls fresh out of high school beginning their working lives.

Women who were employed in the rubber factories were as patriotic as the next person, but they were also motivated by economic considerations. Female rubber workers were well paid—the best paid in any industry in the state. Notwithstanding the stories in the city's newspapers, few women planned to give up these good-paying production jobs at the end of the war—and they had no real reason to expect that they would be forced out. After all, the rubber industry had a long tradition of employing women in production. The large number of women who filed for unemployment, as well as those who attempted to find jobs through the USES, reflected their determination to continue working after the war. Rosie of the rubber factories was not prepared to go back to the home.

(*Opposite*) During the Korean War, BFG women were again making gas masks. This picture, taken on December 17, 1951, shows women making gas-mask covers. *B. F. Goodrich Collection.*

(*Above*) BFG women also made life rafts during the Korean War. *B. F. Goodrich Collection.*

Few permanent changes followed the war. Women rubber workers continued to work at jobs defined by gender. This gender segregation had been altered momentarily in World War I, when a limited number of women took over men's jobs. That segmentation had been reimposed after the armistice was signed. The segmentation had survived the Roaring '20s and the Great Depression. In general, it also survived World War II. Only a minority of the women held men's jobs during the war, and neither the companies nor the union were proponents for women's rights to retain those high-paying jobs.

That should not have been surprising. The women rubber workers always remained outside the power structure of the factory and the union. They had little input into the union, management, or government departments that oversaw production or labor. In this industrial paternalism, men—white men—defined the jobs, determined which women would get the high-paying men's jobs and mediated the disputes. Women working in this environment may have been outside the authority loop, but they developed a network of family and friends who enhanced the quality of the work environment. This did not suddenly happen during World War II, but this had been the case as one generation of women introduced the next to rubber factory work.

There was one new addition to the picture—a permanent addition. African American women had worked in the rubber factories for some time before the war, primarily in maintenance and janitorial jobs. During World War II African American women were introduced into production work, and they never left it.

Socially, the war had brought few permanent changes. Married women continued their traditional responsibilities, even as they worked forty-eight hours a week in the rubber factories. The new evening hours offered by many of the stores and banks helped ease the problems associated with some of their household tasks. The greatest problem facing these married women was child care. Because neither the union, the company, nor the community was ready to face that challenge, women workers themselves had to solve the problem. Again they looked to their network of relatives and friends for help with child care. The much ballyhooed day-care centers opened during the war handled relatively few of the children of these women rubber workers.

Single women found that Akron accorded them much freedom—and the rubber factories gave them the money to fully enjoy that freedom. Akron "roared" on Saturday night—and most of the other nights of the week as well. The city lit up with nightclubs, bars, and dances. It was a great life, if you were young and single and had the money to spend.

Rosie was the third generation of women who worked in Akron's rubber factories. Anna was part of the first generation, when few laws and regulatory agencies protected Ohio's women factory workers. Nonetheless, she found supportive networks of friends and relatives to help her through the ten- to twelve-hour days.

Mildred followed Anna into the rubber factories and benefited from the protective labor legislation that limited women's workday to nine hours and the corporate decision to limit the workday to eight hours. She also enjoyed the dining rooms, the factory infirmaries, the rest rooms, and the other benefits that the rubber companies offered their female employees—and eventually extended to the men in their employ. Mildred and Rosie shared similar experiences. Both suffered through a war; a few workers in each generation were able to take over men's jobs during the course of the wars. But after the war, the women workers of both generations found that they had to give up these well-paid jobs and no one would support their attempts to retain those positions. Mildred and her generation had no union to take up their cause. Rosie and her generation had a union—but it was not willing to take their side on this important issue. After the war, both Mildred and Rosie faced layoffs. But, just as Mildred discovered, Rosie found that she would not be displaced—women would retain their important role in production in the rubber industry.

Rosie the Rubber Worker was following patterns established two generations before. World War II had changed little. Her gender-segregated environment at work remained the same; her network of friends and relatives remained the key element to understanding her life within the factory—and outside it.

appendix

Interviews

Many women shared their reminiscences with the author through interviews or in written form. It is their reminiscences that provide the richness of this book. The author wishes to thank the following women for all the reminiscences, input, and time they gave during the preparation of this book:

Dorothy (Chevin) Bailey

Verna Nadine Barrett

Isabel (Moran) Bittner

Dorothy Bolen

Thelma (Moore) Bolen

Anna M. (Hull) Burnside

Beulah "Billie" (Schott) Cardarelli

Almeda (Bell) Cole

Ruby C. Donnelly

Phyllis I. Douglas

Mildred (Zelei) Eakin

M. Lucrete (Arrington) Endres

Grace O. (Hanlon) Fannin

Cecilia "Sally" Foore

Gladys (Burton) Gibson

Inez (Rogers) Gindraw

Agnes Lackney

Cordelia Lett

Tressie McGee

Sandra Mondrich

Anna Nebereczny

Frances P. (Golliday) Olechnowicz

Margaret (Cooney) O'Leary

Ottie Phillips

Betty Sladden Pinter

Josephine Reese

Dorothy Rightmyer

Ernestine Rogers

Dolly (Bell) Rometo

Mary B. Sitko

Clarice E. Douglas Smith

Mary E. Smith

Margaret B. (Crock) Wagner

Mildred (Homan) Young

Bibliography

Manuscript Collections

Bierce Library, Archives, University of Akron, Akron, Ohio
    B. F. Goodrich Collection, Archives, Bierce Library
    Firestone Tire and Rubber Company Collection
    Goodyear Tire and Rubber Company Collection
    Summit County Historical Society Collection
    United Rubber Workers International Union Collection
    United Rubber Workers Union Local Five Collection
    Young Women's Christian Association, Akron Chapter, Collection
Cleveland State University Library, Cleveland, Ohio
    Cleveland Press Collection
National Archives, Washington D.C.
    War Production Board Collection
    Women's Bureau Collection

Newspapers

Akron Beacon and Republican
Akron Beacon Journal
Akron Times-Press
B. F. Goodrich *Circle*
B. F. Goodrich *War Production News*
Cleveland Plain Dealer

Cleveland Press
Firestone *Non-Skid*
Goodyear *Wingfoot Clan*
Goodyear *Wingfoot Clan Aircraft*
United Rubber Worker
United Rubber Worker The Airbag

Government Documents

Baker, H. C. "History of the Akron District Board of War Production Board." Policy D File 077.1, no date.

Civilian Production Administration. *Industrial Mobilization for War: History of the War Production Board and Predecessor Agencies, 1940–1945.* Vol. 1: *Program and Administration.* 1941. New York: Greenwood Press, 1969.

Department of Commerce, Bureau of Census. *Fifteenth Census of the United States, 1930: Population.* Vol. 1: *Number and Distribution of Inhabitants. . . .* Washington, D.C.: Government Printing Office, 1931.

———. *Fifteenth Census of the United States: 1930, Unemployment.* Vol. 2: *General Report United States.* Washington, D.C.: Government Printing Office, 1932.

———. *Fourteenth Census of the United States Taken in the Year 1920.* Vol. 2: *Population 1920: General Reports and Analytical Tables.* Washington, D.C.: Government Printing Office, 1922.

———. *Fourteenth Census of the United States Taken in the Year 1920.* Vol. 9: *Manufacturers 1919: Reports for States, with Statistics for Principal Cities.* Washington, D.C.: Government Printing Office, 1923.

———. *A Report of the Seventeenth Decennial Census of the United States. Census of Population: 1950.* Vol. 2: *Characteristics of the Population: Number of Inhabitants, General and Detailed Characteristics of the Population. Part 1, United States Summary.* Washington, D.C.: Government Printing Office, 1953.

———. *A Report of the Seventeenth Decennial Census of the United States: Census of Population, 1950.* Vol. 2: *Characteristics of the Population, Part 33, Ohio.* Washington, D.C.: Government Printing Office, 1952.

———. *Sixteenth Census of the United States: 1940 Population.* Vol. 3: *The Labor Force: Occupation, Industry Employment, Income, Part 4, Nebraska-Oregon.* Washington, D.C.: Government Printing Office, 1943.

———. *Sixteenth Census of the United States: 1940. Manufactures 1939.* Vol. 2: Part 2. Washington, D.C.: Government Printing Office, 1942.

———. *Thirteenth Census of the United States Taken in the Year 1910.* Vol. 4: *Population 1910, Occupational Statistics.* Washington, D.C.: Government Printing Office, 1914.

———. *Thirteenth Census of the United States Taken in the Year 1910.* Vol. 3: *Population 1910, Reports by States with Statistics for Counties, Cities and Other Civil Divisions.* Washington, D.C.: Government Printing Office, 1913.

Department of Commerce and Labor, Bureau of Census. *Special Reports: Occupations at the Twelfth Census*. Washington, D.C.: Government Printing Office, 1904.

———. *Thirteenth Census of the United States Taken in the Year 1910*. Vol. 9: *Manufacturers 1909: Reports by States with Statistics for Principal Cities*. Washington, D.C.: Government Printing Office, 1912.

Department of Interior, Office of the Census. *Census Reports*. Vol. 2: *Twelfth Census of the United States Taken in the Year 1900, Population Part 1*. Washington, D.C.: Census Office 1902.

———. *Census Reports*. Vol. 7: *Twelfth Census of the United States Taken in the Year 1900, Manufacturers Part 1, United States by Industries*. Washington, D.C.: Census Office, 1902.

———. *Census Reports, Vol. 8: Twelfth Census of the United States Taken in the Year 1900, Manufacturers Part 2, States and Territories*. Washington, D.C.: Census Office, 1902.

———. *Compendium of the Eleventh Census: 1890 Part 1, Population*. Washington, D.C.: Government Printing Office, 1892.

———. *Compendium of the Eleventh Census: 1890 Part 2, Vital and Social Statistics*. Washington, D.C.: Government Printing Office, 1894.

———. *Compendium of the Tenth Census (June 1, 1880)*. Washington, D.C.: Government Printing Office, 1883.

———. *Ninth Census* Vol. 3: *The Statistics of the Wealth and Industry of the United States*. Washington, D.C.: Government Printing Office, 1872.

Department of Labor, Bureau of Labor Statistics. *The Boot and Shoe Industry in Massachusetts as a Vocation for Women*. Washington, D.C.: Government Printing Office, 1918.

———. *Handbook of Labor Statistics*. Bulletin 916, 147th ed. Washington, D.C.: Government Printing Office, 1948.

———. *Wages in Rubber Manufacturing Industry August 1942*. Bulletin 737. Washington, D.C.: Government Printing Office, 1943.

Department of Labor, Women's Bureau. *The American Woman: Her Changing Role, Worker, Homemaker, Citizen*. Bulletin 224. Washington, D.C.: Department of Labor, 1948.

———. *Changes in Women's Occupations, 1940 to 1950*. Washington, D.C.: Government Printing Office, 1954.

———. *Choosing Women for War Industry Jobs*. Special Bulletin 12. Washington, D.C.: Government Printing Office, 1943.

———. *Effective Industrial Use of Women in the Defense Program*. Special Bulletin 1. Washington, D.C.: Government Printing Office, 1940.

———. *Employed Mothers and Child Care*. Bulletin 246. Washington, D.C.: Government Printing Office, 1953.

———. *Employment of Women in the Early Post War Period: With Background of Prewar and War Data*. Washington, D.C.: Government Printing Office, 1946.

———. *Negro Women War Workers*. Bulletin 265. Washington, D.C.: Women's Bureau, Department of Labor, 1945.

———. *The New Position of Women in American Industry.* Bulletin 12. Washington, D.C.: Government Printing Office, 1920.

———. *The Occupational Progress of Women, 1910 to 1930.* Bulletin 104. Washington, D.C.: Government Printing Office, 1933.

———. *The Occupational Progress of Women, 1910 to 1930.* Bulletin 104-A. Washington, D.C.: Government Printing Office, 1940.

———. *Safety Clothing for Women in Industry.* Special Bulletin 3. Washington, D.C.: Government Printing Office, 1941.

———. *Technological Changes in Relation to Women's Employment.* Bulletin 107. Washington, D.C.: Government Printing Office, 1935.

———. *When You Hire Women.* Special Bulletin 14. Washington, D.C.: Government Printing Office, 1944.

———. *Women's Wartime Hours of Work: The Effect of Their Factory Performance and Home Life.* Bulletin 208. Washington, D.C.: Government Printing Office, 1947.

Department of Labor and War Production Board. "Condensed Proceedings of the Conference on Health Hazards in the Rubber Industry." Akron, Ohio, May 29, 1942.

Edwards, Alba M. *Sixteenth Census of the United States: 1940 Population, Comparative Occupation Statistics for the United States, 1870 to 1940.* Washington, D.C.: Government Printing Office, 1943.

Hill, Joseph A. *Women in Gainful Occupations, 1870 to 1920.* Census Monographs 9. Washington, D.C.: Government Printing Office, 1929.

Marquardt, Philomena and Sophia F. McDowell. *Seniority in the Akron Rubber Industry July 1944.* Washington, D.C.: Bureau of Labor Statistics, Department of Labor, 1945.

Pidgeon, Mary Elizabeth. *Changes in Women's Employment During the War.* Special Bulletin 20. Washington, D.C.: Government Printing Office 1944.

———. *A Preview as to Women Workers in Transition from War to Peace.* Special Bulletin 18. Washington, D.C.: Government Printing Office, 1944.

Sumner, Helen L. *Report on Condition of Women and Child Wage-Earners in the United States in 19 Volumes,* Volume 9: *History of Women in Industry in the United States, A Report to the United States Senate, 61st Congress, 2nd Session.* Document 645. Washington, D.C.: Government Printing Office, 1910.

Books and Articles

Allen, Hugh. *The House of Goodyear: Fifty Years of Men and Industry.* Cleveland: Corday and Gross, 1949.

———. *Rubber's Home Town: The Real-Life Story of Akron.* New York: Stratford House, 1949.

Anderson, Karen. *Wartime Women: Sex Roles, Family Relations and the Status of Women During World War II.* Westport, Conn.: Greenwood Press, 1981.

Babcock, Glenn D. *History of the United States Rubber Company: A Case Study in Coop-

eration Management. Indiana Business Report 39. Bloomington: Bureau of Business Research, Graduate School of Business, Indiana University, 1966.

Babin, Nancy Felice. "Women Auto Workers and the United Automobile Workers' Union (UAW-CIO), 1935–1955." Ph.D. dissertation, University of Michigan, 1984.

Blasio, Mary Ann. "Akron and the Great Depression: 1929–1933." M.A. thesis, University of Akron, 1987.

Braybon, Gail, and Penny Summerfield. *Out of the Cage: Women's Experiences in Two World Wars.* London: Pandora Press, 1987.

Chafe, William H. *The American Woman: Her Changing Social, Economic, and Political Roles, 1920 to 1970.* London: Oxford University Press, 1972.

Connor, Harry. "Collective Bargaining by United Rubber Workers." *Monthly Labor Review* (September 1939): 607.

Derber, Milton. "The New Deal and Labor." *The New Deal: The National Level.* Vol.1, edited by John Braeman, Robert H. Bremmer, and David Brody. Columbus: Ohio State University Press, 1975.

Douty, H. M. "Wages in Rubber and Tube Plants, August 1942." *Monthly Labor Review* (February 1943) 249–50.

Drucker, Mary J. *The Rubber Industry in Ohio: Occupational Study No. 1.* State Vocational Guide. December 1937.

Foner, Philip S. *Women and the American Labor Movement.* New York: Free Press, 1979.

———. *Women and the American Labor Movement: From World War I to Present.* New York: Free Press, 1980.

———, ed. *The Factory Girls.* Urbana: University of Illinois Press, 1977.

Grismer, Karl H. *Akron and Summit County.* Akron: Summit County Historical Society, 1952 [?].

Hartmann, Susan. *The Home Front and Beyond: American Women in the 1940s.* Boston: Twayne, 1982.

Hazard, Blanche Evans. *The Organization of the Boot and Shoe Industry in Massachusetts Before 1875.* Cambridge, Mass.: Harvard University Press, 1921.

Heacock, Nan. *Battle Stations!: The Home Front World War II.* Ames: Iowa State University Press, 1992.

Hirshfield, Deborah. "Rosie Also Welded: Women and Technology in Shipbuilding During World War II." Ph.D. dissertation, University of California-Irvine, 1987.

Honey, Maureen. *Creating Rosie the Riveter: Class, Gender and Propaganda During World War II.* Amherst: University of Massachusetts Press, 1984.

Kesselman, Amy. *Fleeting Opportunities: Women Shipyard Workers in Portland and Vancouver During World War II and Reconversion.* Albany: State University of New York Press, 1990.

Knepper, George W. *Akron, City at the Summit.* Tulsa, Okla.: Continental Heritage Press 1981.

———. *Ohio and Its People.* Kent, Ohio: Kent State University Press, 1989.

Lief, Alfred. *The Firestone Story: A History of the Firestone Tire and Rubber Company.* New York: Whittlesey House, 1951.

Lingeman, Richard. *The American Home Front, 1941–1945*. New York: G. P. Putnam's Sons, 1970.

Litchfield, P. W. *Industrial Voyage: My Life as an Industrial Lieutenant*. Garden City, N.Y.: Doubleday, 1954.

Milkman, Ruth. *Gender at Work: The Dynamics of Job Segregation by Sex during World War II*. Urbana: University of Illinois Press, 1987.

Nelson, Daniel. *American Rubber Workers and Organized Labor, 1900–1941*. Princeton: Princeton University Press, 1988.

Nicholls, William H., and John A. Vieg. *Wartime Government in Operation*. Philadelphia: Blakiston, 1943.

O'Brien, Kenneth Paul, and Lynn Hudson Parsons, eds. *The Home-Front War: World War II and American Society*. Westport, Conn.: Greenwood Press, 1995.

O'Reilly, Maurice. *The Goodyear Story*. Elmsford, N.Y.: Benjamin, 1983.

Pesotta, Rose. *Bread Upon the Waters*. Ithaca, N.Y.: ILR Press, New York State School of Industry and Labor Relations, Cornell University, 1987.

Regli, Adolph C. *Rubber's Goodyear: The Story of a Man's Perseverance*. New York: Julian Messner, 1941.

Roberts, Harold Selig. *The Rubber Workers: Labor Organization and Collective Bargaining in the Rubber Industry*. New York: Harper and Bros., 1944.

Robinson, Harriet H. *Loom and Spindle*. Kailua, Hawaii: Press Pacifica, 1976.

The Rubber Industry and the War. N.p.: Rubber Manufacturers Association, n.d.

"The Rubber Trade in Akron." *India Rubber World* (December 1, 1905): 94.

Rupp, Leila. *Mobilizing Women for War: German and American Propaganda, 1939–1945*. Princeton: Princeton University Press, 1978.

Sufrin, Sidney. "Earnings in the Manufacture of Rubber Products, May 1940." *Monthly Labor Review* (June 1941): 1490–1507.

Sypher, A. H. "Plastic Rubber's Growing Pains." *Nation's Business* (January 1944): 42–50.

Test, Edna Moore. "Occupations for Women in Akron: A Study of Stores, Public Utilities, and Factories." M.A. thesis, Teachers College, University of Akron, June 1929.

Weatherford, Doris. *American Women and World War II*. New York: Facts on File, 1990.

Wise, Nancy Baker, and Christy Wise. *A Mouthful of Rivets: Women at Work in World War II*. San Francisco: Jossey-Bass, 1994.

Wolf, Ralph F. *India Rubber Man: The Story of Charles Goodyear*. Caldwell, Ida.: Caxton Printers, 1939.

"Woman's Work in Rubber Factories." *India Rubber World* (November 1, 1905): 42.

Index

McGee, Tressie (*cont.*) conditions and, 85–86; reason for leaving job, 118; uniforms and, 102
McIntosh, Mary, 126
McKain, Dove, 35–36
McKinney, Ellen, *49*
McLaughlin, Claire, *154*
Mallis, Grace, 47
Manderbach, Elizabeth, 53
Manual dexterity, 12, 20, 76
Marathon Tire company, 13
Martin, Nancy, *154*
Marital status, 38, 122
Markle, Dorothy F., 100, 127
Markle, Harry, 59, 88, 117, 127, 150
Marriage, 7, 42, 147; traditional behaviors and, 16; work and, 4, 20, 43
Married women, 16, 18, 44; child care and, 158; divorce rate and, 132–33; friendship networks of, 131–32; housework and, 129; layoffs and, 34–35, 41, 48; part-time work and, 67; pressure to give up jobs, 36, 37–38; turnover rates and, 117
Mason Rubber Company, 13
Mears, Lucilla, *95*
Mears, Stella, 123
Mechanization, 20
Men, 20, 25, 154; absenteeism rate of, 114; harassment of women workers, 105; hostility to women in workplace, 93; as labor recruiters, 65; living costs and, 34; seniority and, 91; as supervisors, 103; unemployment of, 36; wages of, 41, 96; work environment and, 95; working conditions and, 96
Metropolitan Housing Authority, 16, 128
Metz, Lena, 20–21
Mikesell, Mrs. Robert, 5
Miller Rubber Company, 12, 25, 77
Minto, Dorothy, 141
Mobile housing, 140–41
Mohawk Rubber Company, 13
Money, motivation and, 8, 16, 19, 68
Moneypenny, Ann, 56
Moore, Thelma, 57, 69, 135
Moran, Isabel, 69, 91, 102, 114; at end of World War II, 146–47; friendship network of, 133

Morgan, Mrs. Gomer, 10
Mothers, 54, 65–66, 122–23, 138, 140, 145
Movie stars, 34
Mowery, Edith, *142, 143*
Mueller, Vera, 5
Murphy, Lillie, 20, 27

Neff, Martha, 152
New England, 11–12
New Jersey, 13
Newspapers, 5, 7, 10, 38; patriotism and, 52; recruitment of workers and, 57–58
Noe, Florence, 32–33, 35
Non-Skid (publication), 7, 34
Norman, Dorothy, 44
Nye, Isabel, 27

Occupational diseases, 98
Office of Civilian Defense (OCD), 125, 126
Office of War Information, 1, 102
Office workers, 7
O'Hara, Edith, 45
Ohio, 13, 15, 24, 154
Olechnowicz, Frances. *See* Golliday, Frances
Olenick, Rosemary, 111
Oliphant, Irene, 69
Oxygen cylinders, 79

Parker, Marjorie, *89*
Partenheimer, Mrs. Arthur, 124
Part-time work, 67
Parvin, Deborah, *101*
Patriarchy, 15, 110–14
Patrick, Norma Jean, 54
Patriotism, 7, 11, 52, 68, 118–19
Patterson, Joan, 98
Pay rates. *See* wages
Payrolls, 14, 36–37, 40
Pence, Grace, 111
Pennsylvania, 33, 39, 65, 154
Perkins, Frances, 151
Pesotta, Rose, 45–46
Petros, Marguerite, *95*
Petty, Winifred, 68
Phillips, Ada, 152
Physical examinations, 65, 66

Seniority, 40–41, 43, 48, 92; end of
    World War II and, 146, 147, 151, 153;
    of men and women, 91
Service dates, 49
Sexual harassment, 26
Shaffer, Blanche, 23–24
Shifts, 124, 127
Shoes, 12, 22, 24, 31, 40
Shopping, 16, 129–31, 130, 155
Shuman, Ann, 93
Silver Squadron, 103, 104
Simek, Ann, 154
Simmons, Maggie, 32, 35
Single women, 16, 38, 61, 120; housing
    for, 137–38; social life in Akron, 136,
    145; wages of, 18
Six-hour day, 17, 94
Sligert, Greta, 121, 122, 133
Slupholm, Anna, 95
Smallwood, Anna, 95
Smith, Amelia, 93
Smith, Ida, 101
Smith, Lola, 116
Smoking, 16, 135–36
Snader, Mary, 5, 7, 93
Snoberg, Ruth, 39
Soapstone, 18, 82
Social clubs, 30, 42, 50, 141
Solvents, 98
Spain, Frances, 118
Spangler, Dessie, 39
Spiker, Red, 105
Sports, 50, 141, 142
Spring, Patricia, 154
Staples, Seaman Elgin, 5
Star Rubber Company, 13
Stephens, Marie, 113
Stereotypes, 68, 155
Stevens, Lucy, 9
Steward, Gwendolyn, 116
Stock market crash (1929), 40
Strader, Guinevere, 55
Strader, Jerry, 55
Strasser, Katherine, 130
Strikes, 19, 97, 107, 110; Industrial
    Workers of the World (IWW) and, 18,
    25, 25–26; United Rubber Workers
    (URW) and, 45–46, 46

Stumfoll, Elizabeth, 101
Summit Beach Park, 137
Sunbathing, 142, 143
Sunday work, 95
Sundries, 12, 31, 48
Sun Rubber Company, 69
Supervisors, 14, 15, 83–84, 103, 108
Sutter, Ruth, 95
Sweet, Dean, 56
Swigart, Esther, 27
Swisher, William, 55

Taylor, Pauline Strader, 55, 123
Tehensky, Anne, 47
Tennissen, Helen, 39
Teter, Gladys, 47
Textile industry, 11–12
Thomas, John, 97–98
Thomas, Nada, 154
Thompson, Mary E., 70
Thorne, Elizabeth, 98
Tot Lot Playgrounds, 128
Toys, 31, 48, 148
Trainer, J. E., 49, 53, 67
Training. See job training
Transportation, 12, 58, 61, 76; absentee-
    ism and, 114; public services for, 130
Troutman, Ida, 39
Tubes, 22, 148
Tumlin, Arlene, 49
Turnover rates, 16, 117–18, 119

Unemployment, 19, 37; end of World
    War II and, 150, 157; of men, 36; of
    women, 44, 52, 58
Uniforms, 82, 101–2
Unions, 17, 43, 91–93, 158, 159; child
    care and, 122, 158; cooperation with
    rubber companies, 64; hours of work
    and, 95–96; male control of, 109–10;
    piecework and, 97; sex differential in
    wages and, 96; workers' family net-
    works and, 56. See also United Rubber
    Workers (URW)
United Rubber Workers (URW), 15, 19,
    44, 46–48, 48, 104; end of World War
    II and, 151; female supervisors and,
    103; formation of, 45; hours of work

and, 94; male dominance in, 109–10; occupational health hazards and, 98; social activities and, 145. *See also* unions

United States Rubber Company, 13

U.S. Employment Services (USES), 32, 53, 56, 63, 68; end of World War II and, 154, 157; recruitment of workers and, 57–58

V-E Day, 113, 146, 151, 152

Ventilation, 18, 28, 98

Victory bonds, *8*

Victory gardens, 142

V-J Day, 147, 151

Vowls, Lula, 33

Vronick, Dolores, *154*

Vulcanization process, 11

Wages, 14, 15, 28, 30, 40, 51; comparison with other industries, 26; gender and, 31; during Great Depression, 41; job training and, 18; minimum, 37; recruitment of workers and, 63, 65, 68; reductions in, 37, 41, 93; sex differential in, 48, 91–92, 96, 109, 155; unions and, 19

Wagner, Mary, 90

Waldeck, Anna, 55

Walker, Helen, 47

Walters, Harry, 54

Walters, Helen, *154*

War Advertising Council, 1

Ward, Ethel, 47

War Labor Board, 91

War Manpower Commission (WMC), 57–61, 63, 88; on absenteeism, 114; child care problem and, 122; end of World War II and, 150; housing shortage and, 136–37; on turnover rates, 117; work environment and, 95

War Production News, 3, 7

Watson, Dorothy, 152

Webb, Edna, 98

Weekends, work on, 95

Weinberg, Betty, 84–85,

Weinberg, Beverly, *154*

Westenbarger, W. D., 56

West Virginia, 33, 39, 55, 121, 135; recruitment drive after World War II, 154; workers recruited from, 61, 65, 66

Whatley, Nina, *154*

White Rubber Company, 69

White women, 16, 23, 38, 55, 62. *See also* women

Wilcox, Mildred, 151

Williams, Anna N., 53–54

Wilson, Lavada, 45

Women, 1, 5, 96; absenteeism rate of, 114; age of rubber workers, 23, 68, 122; community activities and, 143–45; diversity of, 32–33; female culture and patriarchy, 110–14; "female males," 91, 93; female role models, 69; immigrants, 32, 38–39; as inspectors, 5, 9, 21, 34, 77, *109*; male relatives in the service, 7, 8, 9, 54, 151; number of in industrial jobs, 21–22, 25, 77, *78*, 150, 154, 155; opposition to employment of, 22, 37–38, 44–45; prison inmates recruited as workers, 65; reasons for working in rubber factories, 67–69; in shoe industry, 12; social class of, 10; supervised by men, 26–27, 35, 43; as supervisors, 83–84, 96; in textile industry, 11–12; unionization and, 15, 45–48, *48*; as workers in World War I, 14. *See also* African American women; white women

"Women in the War" program, 1

Women's Bureau, 34, 95, 129

Women's jobs, 15, 17, 31, 35, 80–81, *81*, 96

Wood, Velma, *95*

Woodling, Mary, 33

Working conditions, 18, 21, 26, 40, 82–83, 85–86; accidents, 89–90; divorce rate and, 132–33; factory inspectors and, 27–28; hazardous chemicals and ventilation, 98–99; heat, 77, 102, 118; improvement of, 111; male authority and, 96; protective gear and, 89–90; protective labor legislation and, 31; recruitment of workers and, 63

Works Progress Administration (WPA), 49

World War I, 14, 19, 31–33, *33*, 158;

Rosie the Rubber Worker

was designed & composed by Will Underwood in 10.5/15 Janson Text with

Brody EF display type on a Power Macintosh G3 at The Kent State University Press;

printed by sheet-fed offset lithography on 80-pound Fortune Matte stock;

Smyth sewn, bound over binder's boards in Rainbow Odyssey cloth with Rainbow & Multicolor

endpapers, and wrapped with dust jackets printed in four-color process on 100-pound enamel

stock finished with polypropylene matte film lamination by Thomson-Shore, Inc.;

and published by

The Kent State University Press

KENT, OHIO 44242